TO GAIL

-WHERE-
THE SEA
BREAKS

JOHN PREBBLE

RICHARD DREW PUBLISHING
Glasgow

First published 1944
by Secker and Warburg Ltd.

This edition first published 1987 by
Richard Drew Publishing Ltd.
6 Clairmont Gardens
Glasgow G3 7LW
Scotland

British Library Cataloguing in Publication Data

Prebble, John
  Where the Sea Breaks. — (Scottish collection)
  I. Title   II. Series
  823'.912[F]   PR6031.R36

  ISBN 0 86267 178 7

Printed in Great Britain by Blantyre Printing and Binding Co. Ltd.

THEY COME

I

THE wounded bomber came in low over the island and crashed on the hill. Every night the islanders had heard the raiders going over to the mainland, and after dusk the sky was busy with the purposeful traffic of aircraft. This activity was the prelude to invasion, so it was said.

The bomber had been damaged by a fighter three miles off the coast as it was returning, and the second pilot was killed then. The first pilot tried to keep height, but the fighter's fire had destroyed one engine and damaged the other. The plane fell rapidly.

The islanders had heard the sound of it above the wind, but they had grown accustomed to such noises since the war began, and they did not know that the plane had crashed. The clouds were low, lower than the top of the hill itself, and the light of the burning plane was hidden from any that looked out of their windows. They did not know that four airmen had crawled from the wreck and set fire to it.

And the fighter wheeled back to the mainland, not knowing that he had even hit his target.

The storm came up. It was very strong on the night the enemy came to the island.

II

THE pilot was the only officer in the machine. His crew were N.C.Os. He was very young and he had fought in Spain with the Condor Legion before he was twenty. For that a black-and-white medal ribbon was tucked below a button in his tunic. He had been in the *Luftwaffe* for five years and he did not like piloting bombers. He was a fighter pilot, and the first time he had gone into action had been against an old French biplane over Madrid. In this war he had destroyed a Polish cavalry squadron, just across the frontier, and he could still be amused by the memory of the horses falling, their backs broken by the fire from his plane, and the men rolling over and over in the road among the dust. He had allowed the standard bearer to gallop two miles along the road to Warsaw before he had killed him. Such things were exciting, and he did not like piloting bombers, although he had been flying them since the battle for France. He was a fighter pilot, he knew that, and without conceit he could admire the night fighter who shot him down so dexterously.

He sat on a stone in the valley, and as he waited for the light to grow he smoked a cigarette. He smoked rarely, only when he had a problem to solve, and then he inhaled deeply and let the smoke dribble from his mouth. He fixed his eyes on the ashes of the bomber, and was proud of the fact that he had been able to bring it down without injury to the crew, that they had been able to dismantle two of the guns and place them beneath a tarpaulin. It had perhaps seemed a strange thing to do and the navigator had looked as if he would have liked to ask questions, but the pilot had been quite curt and had not invited them. He made the men go to sleep after they had buried what was left of the second pilot, and he stayed awake himself, trying to disentangle his mind from the confusion that had preceded and followed the destruction of his plane.

He was wet. It had not rained during the night, although the wind was high, driving the spray in from the sea and drenching the island. He shivered. He inhaled often and felt the warmth of the smoke curl about his throat.

It was dawn already, and when the pilot had finished his cigarette he aroused the crew. Scraps of purple flowers from the heather were caught in the buttons of their tunics. The pilot looked at them and spoke sharply about them until the men pulled at the flowers nervously and wondered what was to be done next. The valley ringed them about. It was a small hollow, as if a child had scooped out wet sand, and about thirty feet below them a small stream fell down to a gap that led to the sea. They could smell the sea, it was sharp and salty, and the wind brought drops of it to their lips. The valley was in shadow and chill, but all around the crest was the golden fire of the dawn.

The pilot put on his cap. He called the three N.C.Os. to attention and saluted them. In silence he studied them quite carefully. The rear-gunner. He was as young as the pilot and a Party member. His face was round and the hair on his brows almost white, giving his face a look of permanent incredulity. His lips were full and his hands fat. The wireless operator. He was dark, his skin was sallow and blotched. He came from the south and, because he was a Catholic he wore a cross on a gold chain beneath his undershirt, and last night the pilot had heard him praying before he went to sleep. The pilot did not like the wireless operator much, but he envied him the experience of having bombed Rotterdam.

The third man was the navigator, a much older man and the senior N.C.O. He came from the industrial district in the north and had a high, thin head and big hands. He stooped slightly and rarely smiled, except to himself. He was a very good navigator and conscientious. The pilot could rely on him. He was tall, and because his height was disconcerting the pilot was inclined to be brusque with him. His hair was thin and the wind blew it across his face.

The pilot pulled at the edges of his tunic and straightened his shoulders.

"We'd left the mainland when the fighter shot at us," he said, "So I imagine we have landed on an island." He turned to the navigator. "Which one?"

The navigator said, "I don't know, Herr Leutnant." He looked at the blood on his right hand. "The first burst from the fighter tore up my charts and wounded me slightly. But I remember there were one or two small islands on our course in, and we followed approximately the same course out."

The officer looked up at the hills and then at the gap. "That's not good enough. We must know which one."

The navigator moved his shoulders slightly and looked up to the sky and then back at the pilot. "What difference does it make? We are prisoners now. My father was a prisoner last time. It wasn't bad in some ways, he used to say."

"There aren't any prisoners yet." The pilot was stung. "Let it be understood that there are no prisoners yet!"

This time the navigator really did shrug his shoulders, but he said nothing.

"We'll climb up to the top of this valley and see what we can make of this island," said the pilot. "You"—and he motioned to the navigator—"you take that side and the others will come with me." He pulled out his watch. "You have one?"

"Yes, Herr Leutnant."

"Then return here in twenty minutes. I want you to draw me a rough map of what you see from up there. Don't let anyone see you if you can help it."

The navigator saluted and began to climb the side of the hill. Halfway up he stopped and lit a cigarette. The pilot, watching him go, frowned when he saw the sudden flame and the spiral of blue smoke. He pushed the tip of his tongue between his lips in a grimace of irritation, and then closed his mouth tight. He turned about, and, ordering the others to follow him, climbed upwards, grasping the heather with his hands and digging the toes of his boots into the wet soil.

III

IT was a small island, and it stood alone in the sea. It was shaped like a wedge, with a hollow in the centre of the gentle slope. It was there that the bomber had crashed. The wedge sloped away to the east, towards the mainland, and on the steep side, which was almost perpendicular, there was a cliff, high and gashed with dark coves. There the sea was never calm; even at low tide it beat against the rocks and there was no shore to be seen. The spray was flung high into the air, and sometimes the sea-fowl, as they hung above the surf, looked as if they were part of the spray too.

The rocks were black, and the sea, grey in its anger, washed against them until they shone like pitch that had been cut with a knife.

To the top of this cliff the navigator had climbed. He lay

among the rough grass and the heather and looked down at the rocks, or out across the sea to the horizon. Then he took his watch from his wrist and hung it before him on the heather. He took a notebook from his pocket and began to sketch the island, or what he could see of it. When he had finished that he looked at his watch. Ten minutes yet. He lit another cigarette and smiled gently. He lay on the cliff top, with the weight of his body resting on his elbows and the cigarette hanging from his lips.

He had never felt so close to the sea before. Now and then the wind, which seemed to be rising, blew it up from the rocks below to his face. He liked the taste of it. Away from the island, it stretched in restless excitement, scored with white foam. It gave the navigator an impression of great power, and for that he respected its immensity. He was a city dweller and he did not know the sea, but as an airman he knew the weather, and on the horizon behind the wind he saw the darkness and obese bellies of the storm clouds. And below them the sea moved in anticipation.

He felt pleased at being alone. He had not been alone for a long time, and this was strange to him. He became conscious of thoughts and feelings that had long lain dormant, and their revival was almost embarrassing. He tried to avoid it by fastening his attention on what was going on about him, to lose himself that way. Now and then, with a sad skirl, a gull would rise up from the cliff below, circle above him and so near that he could see the open, orange beak and the black eyes, and then the bird would drop swiftly to the rocks. If only men could fly like that, he thought, and in a sudden vivid image he visualised an air force with such power—bombers, fighters, dive-bombers. He liked such semblances of power, for in them he could lose a sense of personal insignificance. First the sea, and now these gulls. He sucked at a heather sprig in between deep inhalations from his cigarette.

He had only three more minutes. He thought of the pilot and the rest of the crew. It was interesting to speculate on what was to happen. It might have been a relief to accept the possibility of being a prisoner, and for the moment his body ached for relief from tension. But they had not taken out the guns for that, nor the belts of cartridges, serpentine and shining. He brushed away the doubts and watched another gull with interest. He did not like the pilot, but the boy was clever, resourceful, and a Party member. He looked out to sea again. The great darkness in the west had come nearer, threatening the whole sky, and beneath it the sea was uneasy.

The navigator looked down at his hands where they rested on his forearms. The third and fourth fingers were trembling, and he could feel the vibration carrying on through his body. He knew why, and in this sudden realisation the thick nausea that had swept over him as the plane had been falling returned. The sickness was bad, and for the moment it was as if he could hear the babble of frenzied voices over the inter-communication telephone, a high, sharp voice above it all (he thought it was the pilot's) shouting, "Stern, *Stern*!" but the second pilot, whose name it was, didn't answer. The wind was rushing through the fuselage, and carrying with it the hot air from the burning engine. Smell of petrol. Smell of blood. The crazy, reeling course of the machine. The wireless operator screaming.

The navigator opened his eyes. There were the sea, the gulls, and the storm-wind on his face.

In the plane he had not felt like this, he thought: he had been calm, trying to salvage the charts. Perhaps he had not thought the plane would crash: he trusted the pilot. But no, he remembered the downward plunge of it, the darkness and horror, and then the crash, the noise fading away into the silence of the wind. The rain on his face, and he wondering whether he was the only one alive, whether he *was* alive. Vomiting suddenly into the wet earth.

There had been danger before, above the patchwork Flemish fields, the sandy beaches of North France. But always the reassurance that below, behind, were friends.

Now, and he realised it as he looked out to the sea, up at the gulls that watched him coldly, he and the others were alone, quite alone. He gripped his arms to stop the trembling of his fingers.

It was cold. The navigator turned up the collar of his tunic, and the cloth rasped against his unshaven chin. But the scene was fascinating, and he stayed to watch it, to drag his mind from the memory of the crash. Up with the spray the wind blew the birds. They hawked and swooped above him, watching with stony eyes, and beaks open. He looked at them quietly, and then guffawed. Planes that hung in the air like that would soon be shot down, and he expressed his sudden contempt by throwing heather at them. But the wind tore it away almost before it left his hand.

He got up and strapped on his watch. Standing there, he could see down the hill, and beyond the ridge on the other side of the hollow. Immediately he became aware of the village there on the shore at the bottom of the slope, and he dropped to the heather again, out of sight, his back to the sea.

On the other side of the hollow, three figures lay in the heather, watching the village.

The pilot studied the cottages through his field glasses. There were about five or six of them, so far as he could see, a roll in the earth hid them from a fuller view. They were long and low, painted white and with roofs that were thatched with turf in some part and tiled in others. There were chimneys at either end of the houses, made of crude, undressed stones, and at least one in each house was smoking. All occupied, thought the lieutenant, and began to docket away in his mind the conclusions he drew from what he could see. All of the houses, except one, were grouped in a rough semicircle about what seemed to be a rude jetty of great stones. The other house stood out in front of them, alone, facing them with its back to the jetty, and its single door and three small windows looked at the other houses.

The jetty behind it went out for a few yards into deep water, and there it ended in a jumble of stones. Above it stood a lamp standard without a lantern. And on either side the beach stretched for about half a mile, strong shingle on which the waves pounded, ending in great boulders which were platforms for the gulls.

The lieutenant fastened his glasses on four black objects drawn up on the beach. He sucked in his lower lip and gripped it tightly with his teeth.

"Boats!" he said softly.

He studied each boat carefully and slowly released his lip; there were white marks where his teeth had gripped. Then he turned his glasses on each house again. At the last, the house that stood sentinel-like before the others, he lowered the glasses sharply.

"Radio!"

The lieutenant kept staring at the houses, tapping on his glasses with the fingers of his right hand. The nails were long and clean and the noise they made was distinct. First a rapid beat with the first finger, then the second, then the third, then the fourth, and then perhaps all together. No one seemed to be moving in the village, until, although it was early, a woman came out of the nearest house and began to hang some washing on the line. The wind filled the clothes and made of them gross caricatures of limbs and torsos. The rear-gunner splayed out his fat hands and whispered to the wireless operator and they both looked quickly at the women and laughed obscenely.

The pilot frowned. "Hart!"

"Yes, Herr Leutnant?" said the rear-gunner.

"Go down to the wreck and meet Mann, and both of you come up here with the guns." He picked up his glasses and began to study the village again. He looked at the woman, stuck out his lower lip, and then bit at it and passed on to the boats. He felt the wind blowing against the back of his neck, catching up the tail of his tunic and becoming each instant more and more forceful. But in front of him the sun was brilliant, and dappling the waves far out to the horizon. He could not see that the storm was coming again.

After a while a man came out of one of the houses and walked down to the boats on the shore. He was followed by two children, who played with the stones, and threw them into the sea. The three of them sat on one of the boats, on the gunwale, for the boat had heeled over when the tide left it. The pilot could hear the children's laughter quite plainly.

And somewhere among the houses a woman was singing. Perhaps it was the woman who had hung out the washing, for it was a young voice and pleasing.

Some fifteen minutes later another man came out from the houses. A black-and-white collie was before him, running with its long hair waving at its flanks, and a tail that bobbed and streamed out like a pennant. Its master was an old man with a grey bonnet on his head. He had a white beard, and a stick on which he leant as he began to climb the hill.

The lieutenant reached a hand down to his side and loosened his pistol holster.

He kept his glasses on the man.

Behind the houses, up the slope for some hundred yards or so stretched a few rough enclosures, walled about with great slabs of stone. In the lower fields were garden vegetables, the bushy clumps of potatoes and yellow stalks of decaying cabbages, and here and there a few clumps of rough flowers, golden and brown chrysanthemums that flamed against the black earth. And in the higher fields there was nothing but the ridges of ploughed earth, overgrown with long grass.

The old man came no higher than the last cultivated field. He leaned there on a wall, with his coat brushing the yellow flowers, and he filled his pipe while the collie rushed about him among the tufts.

The woman had stopped singing, and the children were on their knees by the boat, piling stones one upon the other. The airmen could hear the clitter of the stones as they rolled down the pile, and other sounds, voices, indistinct, and the fat, complacent clucking of chickens.

Then there was the sound of metal and footfalls behind them and the lieutenant turned quickly and put his finger to his lips as Mann and the rear-gunner came up the hill. They stopped and stood there in the heather, leaning forward slightly. Each carried a dismantled gun, and a wreath of machine-gun bullets about his neck. Their mouths were open and they were breathing heavily. Motioning them to be quiet, the pilot beckoned them on. They laid the guns in the heather below the ridge and dropped beside the other two airmen. They stared at the houses with interest.

"Mann!"

"Yes, Herr Leutnant?"

The pilot slithered down from the ridge and sat upright. The navigator joined him.

"You speak English, Mann?"

"Yes, Herr Leutnant."

"Good." The pilot looked at him curiously, but said nothing.

He took a cigarette case from his pocket and offered one to the navigator. He did not take one himself.

"What did you discover?"

"We are on an island, Herr Leutnant. About four miles square, I should say, and mostly rock. To the west there, look I've drawn it here, it's a sheer drop of two to three hundred feet. Nothing could land or leave from there." He placed a finger on the contours. The lieutenant looked at the broken nail with distaste and pulled the map away from it. He looked at the drawing carefully.

"Good. Any sign of life that side?"

"Only wild life, Herr Leutnant."

The pilot looked at him sharply. "Listen to me carefully, Mann. We shall take possession of this island. It would be ridiculous to surrender to a handful of old men and women. Until we can make contact with whatever of our forces have landed on the mainland, we shall stay here. It should be easy; nothing can stop us."

The navigator glanced at the guns.

"Those can be mounted to suit our requirements," said the pilot. "But they have a radio down there and we must settle with that first."

The navigator felt a touch of admiration. He thought of the gulls and the grey power of the sea rolling. And as he thought of the sea he said:

"Herr Leutnant!"

"What is it?"

"There's bad weather coming. You can see it from up there. It'll be very bad, I think."

The pilot pursed his lips. "Not very serious. Perhaps it's all to the good. If it's very bad there'll be no visitors until we're ready. Put your cigarette out and come up here. And, Mann!"

"Yes, Herr Leutnant?"

"You will only smoke when I give you permission. Realise that we're as good as at the front."

"Yes, Herr Leutnant!"

The four airmen lay on the ridge watching the village again. The pilot looked at the lonely house for a long time through his glasses. The radio mast worried him. Its thin antennae swayed above the chimney, pointing to the mainland. The navigator was watching the children on the shore, and he thought of his own son. Since he went to France, he had not been home, and he wondered what the boy was looking like now. He was five, no six. Going to school. And the navigator thought of his wife too and wondered about her. He would have liked to pull out a photograph of them both and look at it.

The woman came out to look at the clothes once more and the rear-gunner raised his head and stared at her. He would have liked to borrow the glasses. He whispered again to the Catholic, who flushed. Suddenly the rear-gunner stiffened, raised himself slightly and looked over the grass.

"Herr Leutnant!" he whispered harshly.

"What is it, Hart?"

"There's somebody coming up the hill."

The pilot heard a dog barking, quite near. He looked through the heather and down the hill. He could see no one but the old man, leaning on the wall and looking out to sea. He raised his eyebrows at the rear gunner, who whispered:

"Just below us, Herr Leutnant."

The pilot looked; within fifteen yards the earth folded as a blanket might do, and just above the fold he saw a child's head. The hair was fair, long, and blown up above a round head. The lieutenant turned the palm of his hand down and thrust it toward the earth. He touched his pistol again. The airmen flattened themselves on the ground and Mann found himself looking at the coarse tendrils of heather roots, and the minute insects that poured over them. There were two children in front of the group. The pilot could see them plainly, they were talking quickly and gesticulating in their play. The collie, which the men had seen earlier with the old man, jumped and leaped about the children with a long tongue hanging from the side of its mouth.

The children moved across the slope of the hill, across the airmen's front, and slowly climbed to the ridge a little to their right. The collie trotted along towards the airmen, its eyes sharp and the wind blowing its hair about its belly. It saw them and stopped, panting slightly, with its tail still. Men and dog looked at each other. The pilot had one hand still on his holster and began to take out the weapon.

The children were shouting and the dog turned its head and grinned at them. Its tail moved once or twice, slowly, for it was puzzled by the sight of the airmen. But the children were shouting because they had seen the burnt wreckage of the plane and they were tumbling down the slope to it. The pilot looked at the rear-gunner and nodded at the dog. Hart clicked his fingers and called softly. The animal did not move at first, but then it trotted cautiously across to the gunner, who began to rub its ears, its flanks, and its belly.

The pilot stood up. He grasped his pistol by the barrel and walked behind the dog. He hit it heavily on the skull with the butt. The dog's legs splayed out and it collapsed. Its tongue was bitten through and there were little beads of blood between its teeth. The pilot remembered the Polish horses, and he wiped the butt of the gun on the heather.

"We mustn't give them any warning," he said.

"The children have seen us, Herr Leutnant," said Mann.

The pilot looked down into the hollow. The two children were standing by the plane, holding hands and staring up at the men curiously. They had seen the dog killed and were a little frightened.

"They can do us no harm now," he said. "We'll go down. Grun!" He turned to the wireless operator. "Mount one of these guns and train it on the right-hand chimney of that lone cottage there. Keep your eyes on me as I go down, and if I raise my handkerchief I want you to fire a burst into that chimney.

"Yes, Herr Leutnant."

"And when you hear me fire three quick shots, come down the hill with the gun. Understand it all?"

The pilot stood up. He took out his handkerchief and held it in his left hand. In his right was the pistol. He pushed back the safety catch.

"Follow me," he said to the others.

IV

THEY walked down the hill abreast. The lieutenant was in the centre, carrying his handkerchief and the pistol. The heather was still wet with rain and the sun was in their eyes, so they slid and tumbled from the tussocks, and Hart, who was carrying the other gun like a baby across his chest, cursed everything incoherently. Mann was looking at the old man, who still leant against the wall, his back to them and his eyes looking out across the sea. Now and then he would puff out a little ball of smoke, and the wind caught it immediately and sent it rolling down toward the sea, turning it over and over as it grew bigger and bigger until it was invisible. He did not hear the airmen coming.

Mann looked from the old man to the waves of shining grass and heather. With the rain upon them, they rippled right down the hill to where the walls began, one after the other.

It won't be long now, thought Mann; someone is going to get a shock. He was wondering what the old man would do, and he glanced at the pilot. The officer was looking at the cottage with the radio mast, and beside him Hart stumbled and swore, with interest in nothing but the weight of the gun.

"Can't you carry this thing?" he said to Mann. His face was red and there were little drops of moisture on his eyebrows. Mann did not answer. Like the lieutenant, he too had drawn his pistol and when Hart spoke he pushed forward the safety catch.

The old man turned with a whistle on his lips; he wanted his dog. The airmen were ten yards from him and he looked at them in amazement. Mann smiled at his expression; they had looked like that in Norway and France. It was amusing, but you had to feel a little sorry for them; they couldn't, of course, understand. This old man must have been seventy, his face was brown above a blue jersey, and below his open mouth there was the white beard.

Hart had stopped and was looking at the man sullenly. Mann suspected that he had really stopped to relieve the weight of the gun, but the lieutenant called him abruptly and Hart staggered forward again. Together they went on past the islander, and

Mann could feel the blue-white eyes, wide with amazement, centred between his shoulder-blades.

That had been easy, but the old man could have done nothing, anyway.

They were walking more quickly now, the slope was gentler, and they passed by the cottage where the washing was hanging. Inside the woman was singing again. Mann liked the voice; it was fresh, and he wondered what the song was. Hearing footsteps, the woman stopped singing and called out a question. Hart darted a look at the door and swore at the gun.

The lieutenant broke into a trot. He was running for the isolated house where the radio mast stood. His boots kicked at the cobbles. Up the hillside the old man began to shout and whistle. Mann, running behind his officer, looked back over his shoulder. The old man was a ridiculous figure, waving a stick and raising one leg after the other. Out of the cottage came a woman. She was young, and, wiping her hands automatically on a cloth, she looked at the three airmen with the same incredulous look that the old man had had. She was pretty.

Then she dropped the cloth and shouted. She turned her head and looked up the hill. She began to call some names. Mann recognised them as children's names. He looked forward. The lieutenant had reached the door of the hut. Raising one foot, he kicked at it, and it fell inward and he went inside.

There was the sound of a shot before Mann reached the door. The report sounded very loud, and a little blue smoke puffed itself gently from the cottage.

A dog began to bark.

When Mann went inside he found a little room with a low ceiling that darkened the place. The room was full of furniture, and in one corner there was a radio set, an old-fashioned thing with many knobs and wires. The lieutenant stood by the table with feet astride.

The body of a young man was slowly sliding from a chair beside the radio set. When it reached the floor, it rolled over and Mann saw its face. The heavy bullet, in emerging, had torn away the frontal bone of the skull.

"There was no need to have done that," said Mann.

The pilot swung round; his pistol was raised.

"*What do you mean?*" His voice was shriller than usual, and his eyes bright.

"That is only a receiving set," said Mann. "It could transmit nothing. I imagine he was repairing it."

The pilot raised his chin and eased the collar of his tunic about his throat. "If the man was a technician, he might have proved dangerous."

"*Herr Leutnant!*"

It was Hart at the door, he was fumbling with the gun, trying to feed a belt into it. People were coming out of the cottages and running toward the noise of the shot. Up on the hillside the old man was still shouting and waving his stick. The noise of the barking dogs was above all.

"Come outside, Mann," said the lieutenant sharply, and as they pushed past Hart the officer put a hand on his shoulder. "Stop it," he said, "and stand up here beside us."

There were about twelve persons, a mixture of men and women. Some of the women were young, but most of the men were middle-aged; they looked startled. The lieutenant stepped forward and raised his hand. They saw the pistol and stopped.

"Mann, tell them who we are and how we came here."

The navigator told them, but they said nothing.

"Have you told them that, Mann? Now tell them that they must consider themselves under martial law. This island is under occupation. Ask for the leader, the mayor, or whatever he calls himself."

When Mann told them there was another silence; behind them in the cottage he could hear someone sobbing. There was a cough and a man spoke gently to a dog. There was a nervous laugh, and then a woman, her eyes fixed curiously on the cottage behind the airmen, said that they had no mayor, but that her husband, who was coming up from the shore now, was perhaps what they meant by "leader". Mann looked over his shoulder. A man of about sixty, in a blue-knitted jersey and sea-boots, was climbing over the pebbles. Two children, who had been playing by the sea, were following him. They were asking themselves excited questions. The man came up to the group and stood between the islanders and the airmen, glancing from one to the other.

"*Germans!* What was that shot?"

"Our plane crashed here last night," said Mann. "You are to understand that this island is now under our control, and·you must consider yourself under martial law until regular detachments of our forces arrive."

The islander looked at him. Then he laughed shortly.

"Are you daft, man? If your machine crashed here then you're our prisoners. You might as well be made comfortable. Weather's turning bad and there won't be a boat out from the mainland for a few days." He looked concerned. "What was that shot?"

Mann was saved the trouble of answering. There was a scuffling behind him and a woman pushed by until she stood between the two groups. She had been crying and her hair was untidy. She spoke quickly in a high, unreal voice, words that Mann could not follow, and he felt uneasy. He watched the faces of the islanders. Their expressions were stupid, incredulous, and then amazed horror broke through, just as a bubble will break to the surface of water. The crowd shivered.

The man in sea-boots shouted. His face was red with surprise and he raised his fist.

"Why . . .!"

He moved toward the airmen.

The lieutenant let the hand that held the pistol drop to his side. Instead he raised the other, and the white linen that it gripped fluttered above his head. Almost immediately there was a clanging above their heads, like metal striking metal, and from the side of the chimney undressed stone and rough mortar rolled to the ground. Before the noise of the rolling, broken stones had finished the sound of the shots was brought down the hillside with the wind.

Everybody stood still, some looked up the hill. A woman shouted something about her children.

"Tell them about the gun, Mann."

The navigator said that the machine-gun up in the valley could fire accurately into the village. He advised them not to be foolish. They stood there helplessly, and the woman who had run out of her cottage began to sob, falling on her knees until she was crying heavily. The pilot looked irritated.

"Ask them what this island is, Mann?"

"I cannot understand the name, Herr Leutnant. It's not English, but some secondary language. These people are fishing folk."

"How many of them?"

"Fourteen. Fifteen if you count the dead man, Herr Leutnant, and five or six children."

"Good. Tell them to return to their cottages. They are not to step outside. The first to do so will be shot. Say that we shall give them instructions through this man," he motioned to the man in sea-boots, "later in the day. In particular, no one is to attempt to get near the boats." He tapped his thigh nervously with the pistol as Mann spoke to the islanders. "Do they understand?"

"I think so."

"One more thing. They may remove the body of that man from this cottage, or, better still, one of you take it out. We can't trust them. Say that one of the women must come in and get us some food. That's all."

Mann watched the islanders return to their cottages. They moved quite quietly. It had all gone well, so far.

The lieutenant raised his pistol and fired it three times. Some of the villagers turned, but the rest went on. On the hillside Grun stood up and waved in acknowledgement, and the pilot closed his mouth quickly with satisfaction.

"Hart," he said. "Mount that gun in the doorway here, and see that no one attempts to leave those cottages. You've a good field of view, there, and there. I expect you to keep your eyes open."

Hart rubbed his mouth with the back of his hand and set about mounting the gun. He balanced the gun on its mounting expertly. He had balanced it so before the fighter's fire caught the bomber. There had been darkness, and the slip-stream spreading the rain over the gun turret; rubbing had been no good, he still couldn't see. He had fired once, just once, and watched the coloured tracers curve into the night, and then the fighter's fire had poured into the fuselage and the plane went over and down.

He had shouted like the rest, but he hadn't been afraid. Or had it all happened too quickly for him to be afraid? No, it wasn't that; he just hadn't been afraid. The worst thing about it was the darkness and the rotten, filthy smell of oil. The lieutenant brought the plane down well, even if it had given Hart a headache to be flung on the ground. Made you feel sick. One thing for an upset like that was a woman. It always put you right. There was a woman here; she had been singing. . . .

"Keep your eyes open, Hart." The lieutenant was staring at him stiffly, repeating the command with tart impatience.

The rear-gunner straightened his body.

"Yes, Herr Leutnant!"

V

THE man they called Callum had been sent away, and Mann stood to attention by the table. Throughout the whole interview he had stood there, just to the right of the islander and acting as interpreter. The pilot had sat at the table, his hands pressed close together, finger-tip to finger-tip in front of his face, as if he were praying. He had watched the islander's face carefully. And between him and the others was an oil-lamp on the table, its petal-flame cutting deep lines in the officer's face and shining in the buttons of his tunic. When the pilot moved quickly, as he would do in exasperation or satisfaction, the draught dipped the flame of the lamp and long shadows danced on the walls. The lamp stood on an old table-cloth that was worn in some parts, but still bore the rich colour of its embroidered flowers.

It was a long interview and the fire died wearily in the grate. It did not burn coal, but some smoking, cake-like substance, Mann noticed, that filled the air of the little room with sweet scent.

And now the islander had gone and Mann studied his officer carefully. The boy was worried. There were three clefts in his forehead, above his brow, like a cabalistic sign. The medal ribbon tucked in his tunic was quite brilliant, it seemed to be a new one, and Mann wondered if the officer had replaced the old one since they came down here to the cottages.

"What do you think of him?" asked the lieutenant.

"He seemed honest." He knew that the pilot did not want information. He wanted to know what Mann thought, and because of that the navigator felt irritated. "I think he was right about the boats."

"You mean the storm?"

"Yes. The man is right, if they are left where they are the storm will damage them. You can see by the beach that the tide can come up very high."

"Just how long will it last, do you think?"

Mann listened. The wind was high; it moaned about the cottage and the noise of the breakers on the beach was strong. There was rain coming too; occasionally a gust of it was thrown against the window, like a handful of fine gravel on the panes. "It's hard to say. It may last several days, as he said. In that case we'll probably be cut off from the mainland."

The pilot let his fingers fall together, and, with his hands gripped, tapped himself lightly on the chin several times.

"We can't take the risk. If they move the boats, one or more of them may make an attempt to get away. Where they are they can be covered by the gun at the door."

"And if they're damaged, Herr Leutnant?"

"A risk we *shall* take." He pulled out his cigarette case and lit one, inhaling deeply. "Until our forces reach us, we shall stay here." With each word he exhaled little puffs of smoke that took the shape his lips formed. They drifted down the funnel of the lamp and swirled up again to the blackened ceiling. Mann was curious.

"And if they don't come?"

The pilot stared at him. In the silence the smoke from the cigarette passed between them. "They will come, or we shall go to the mainland."

Mann knew he had made a mistake. "Do you expect trouble from these people?" he asked.

"We must be firm. You noticed that man? He didn't argue or bluster; just accepted orders. You've seen them like that in

France and Poland, haven't you? As yet they don't know what's happened; they're slow people. Later, perhaps, they'll cause trouble, we can't say yet. If anything happens, we'll be firm, as firm as possible!" He looked at Mann and narrowed his eyes, dropping them to look at the burning end of his cigarette. "I don't know you very well, Mann. You were new to my crew, and you aren't a Party member, are you? But you seem intelligent, and won't, I think, be foolish. Will you?"

"Thank you, Herr Leutnant, but I'm aware of my duty."

"Quite! Then we needn't worry about that." He spoke briskly and crushed out his cigarette on the base of the lamp. "Let's prepare. Perhaps there won't be much sleep for us. Hart is at the door now with one gun, and Grun must take the other to the jetty, where he can watch the boats. One or other of you will be at each gun during the night. During the day one at the gun before this door might be sufficient. We'll see. Understand?"

Mann straightened his back.

"Right." The officer stopped and inclined his head. "Do you hear anything?"

Mann listened. "They're singing."

"Singing! Who?"

"The islanders, Herr Leutnant."

The pilot looked at him. He was puzzled, and then he laughed. It was a short, boyish laugh, the laugh of someone who wished to be rid of his humour quickly. "They are extraordinary! Why do they sing? After one of their people has been killed, too."

"I don't know."

"It's unimportant, so long as they keep singing. When you go, send in Grun to repair this wireless set. We must have news. As soon as we hear that our forces have been successful we can leave the island, should they not come here. To-morrow, Mann, I want you to discover whether anyone on this island will give us assistance. For that purpose, you must repeat, as I instructed you to tell that man to-night, that our forces have arrived on the mainland."

"Do you think that there'll be anybody like that, Herr Leutnant?"

The pilot smiled. "There's always someone." Then he frowned.

"It was a pity Lieutenant Stern was killed by the fighter. He spoke English too."

Mann stuck out his lower lip. "Am I to understand that I'm not trusted?"

The pilot gently caressed his medal ribbon. "That's not a question I like to be asked, Mann."

"No, Herr Leutnant."

"Go and relieve Hart; he's probably hungry. And tell the woman to bring me some coffee if there is any."

"They have no coffee, Herr Leutnant."

"Damnation! It will have to be tea." He became amicable. "You know Mann, a doctor once told me that tea makes people neurasthenic. Do you think that's what's wrong with the English?"

"*They* say the same about coffee and us, Herr Leutnant."

The pilot frowned. He did not like contradictions. Then he laughed and dismissed it. "You can go, Mann."

Mann stood for a moment outside in the dark room. The door was open, and Hart was sitting there beside the gun. The room smelt sickly from the fumes of a lamp that had gone out. Occasionally the wind rose higher and blew in the smell of the sea and a wisp of rain. Hart cursed, and he snapped open the breech of the gun and closed it again in his irritation. He looked over his shoulder and saw the shadow of Mann behind him.

"Wondered when you were coming. What's been going on in there? It's cold here and nothing happens."

"Something'll happen soon," said Mann. "It always does, doesn't it?"

Hart looked at him curiously. "You don't sound too pleased," he said.

"Never mind that. Did the old man go back."

"Yes. Uncivil sort of lout. Pushed by here with his hands in his pockets and walked over to the cottages. They've been hallelujahing away over there for a quarter of an hour." He swore and his face was wet with perspiration. "I haven't seen a decent-looking woman yet."

"Go and get some sleep," said Mann coldly, "and tell the woman to make some tea for the lieutenant."

"She's gone to bed, or disappeared."

"Then find her, and Grun's got to repair the radio."

Hart got up and stretched himself, scratching his armpits and yawning. "It was better than this in France." He walked away, grumbling.

Mann lit a cigarette and sat behind the gun, looking across the darkness, where the stone and tussocks led to the other cottages. He listened to the singing and heard the notes of a concertina, until the rising of the storm drowned it for a while. The waves fell on the beach, sucking back the stones until they sounded like the rustling fall of debris after an explosion. That, thought Mann, with a touch of regret, was a more familiar sound.

He began to whistle to himself, and after a while he realised that he was whistling the melody that the woman had been singing when they came down the hill.

VI

THE islanders came to Callum's cottage quietly, crouching by the black walls so that Hart, sitting by his gun in the doorway, should not see them. But he was tired, and the wind that swept up the cliff and blew the spray down the slope toward him blinded him. He could see the white outlines of the cottages, no more. Thin wires seemed to have been stretched across the view, and to try to pierce the veil they made was arduous. He despised the islanders, and was not afraid of them. Four men had cowed them.

But they came to Callum's cottage and sat on the chairs and the floor there, and Callum's wife made tea for them. They crowded together so that the heat steamed the moisture from their clothes. They shared what cups there were, passing them from hand to hand, drinking from the saucers thirstily. The old men were smoking, occasionally moving forward to spit into the fire, and the tobbaco smoke curled about the beams of the low ceiling. In the centre of the bare table stood an oil lamp, burning heavily. Greasy, black smoke tipped the flame and painted whorls of soot on the ceiling, but no one thought of turning it down. And on the fire the kettle bubbled, and boiled, and sang. The light that shone on the brassware also shone in the islanders' eyes and it reflected their alarm as they spoke quickly but quietly over the tops of their cups or through the smoke of their pipes. And most of them were thinking of the boy who had been killed and lay now in the room behind them.

They were waiting for Callum to return from the airmen, and while they waited they sang the words of the Hundred and Twenty-ninth Psalm:

> "*Many a time have they afflicted me from my youth.* . . .
> *Yet they have not prevailed against me.*
> *The plowers plowed on my back;*
> *They made long furrows.* . . ."

They sang to the music of a concertina, and while they sang they put down their tea and edged nearer to the fire, looking above it to the picture that hung there. It was an engraving of an impossible storm, and a dismasted vessel that was caught in it. The high waves curved above its decks and they looked like the leaves of fern in a hot summer.

> "*Let them be as the grass upon the housetops,*
> *Which withereth afore it groweth up:*
> *Wherewith the mower filleth not his hand; nor*
> *He that bindeth sheaves his bosom.* . . ."

There were five men and six women there. The men were well over fifty years of age, all but one, who was a boy, and the years had traced their history in the furrows on their foreheads and marked their suffering in the set of their lips. They wore thick jerseys and some had high boots turned down below the knee. They smoked slowly, with the intimacy of friendship. Two woman had brought their babies, wrapped in long shawls of soft wool that went across the women's shoulders and under one armpit. The women's hair was straight and gathered behind their heads, and now and then one of them would push at a loose hair. The babies sucked their fingers and whimpered. Once or twice a man would break off from the singing of the psalm and listen to the wind, his pipe withdrawn from his mouth and held before him, his head cocked sideways, and then his eyes would be lost in the shadows of his drawn brows.

Callum came in, and upon the opening of the door the singing died away, and the concertina, released by one hand, expired in in one ludicrous discord. The islanders looked at Callum and moved toward him a step. He had turned up the collar of his jacket against the wind and his bonnet was pulled over his face until all that could be seen was the length of his chin and the fullness of his lower lip. He pulled his bonnet forward from his head and dropped it on the hearthstone, and for a moment he watched the little spirals of steam rising from it. Then he turned to his wife, and smiled a little grimly.

"Pour me some tea, Mary lass," he said. "It's a cold night out." And he watched his bonnet again, thoughtfully, until it had a little halo of steam above it, and then he moved it from the hearthstone with his toe. Nothing was said as he drank, and the concertina, with a final squeal of protest, was placed away on the shelf.

Then he said quickly, "They're biding here," and dropped his head over his cup again.

He was a tall man, and when he spoke he seemed taller, for his voice was slow, and it seemed to take a long time to reach whoever he was addressing. But for his chin, his face was short, and he had long hands into which the tar had sunk and traced each fold of flesh. He put his cup on the hob and turned to face the islanders, with his hands in his pockets across his stomach, as he always stood, and his head held forward on his chest.

"Oh aye," he said, looking at their faces. "They're biding a while, and they say that their people have made landings on the mainland and that we've lost the war."

"God save us!" said his wife. But he nodded and the islanders looked at him, puzzled.

"How many of them?" It was the old man the airmen had passed on the hill. He still had his stick and he emphasised each word he spoke with an irritable thump on the floor. He seemed impatient with the whole business.

"Four maybe," said Callum. He moved one hand to the pocket of his jacket and took out his pipe. "But they may be more of them. I don't know how many were up there on the braeside."

"Och, it's daft!" said the old man. "I told you the young men should have stayed with us on the island."

Most of the islanders looked at him wearily, but he glared at them and hammered on the floor with his stick again.

"There was only one," said a woman when the noise had stopped. "The bairns saw him. They were up there with Bran and they found the machine those men came in; it was burnt. The man with all the buttons on his fine coat killed Bran. The bairns saw that and afterwards they spoke to the one who was left, and he gave them this coin." She took it out of her pocket and dropped it on the floor by Callum's feet. It was a religious medallion and did not spin as it fell. The old man stepped forward and angrily sent it whirling away with his stick. It rolled under the cupboard. "But then he started firing the gun," said the woman, "and they ran away."

"They've brought the gun down," said Callum. He looked at his pipe. "They'll shoot us, they say, if . . ."

"Daft!" thumped the stick. "We're not the military. Will they be making war on *us*, then?"

A woman moved her baby higher on her breast. "Yon one with the yellow hair and fat hands came," she said in a high voice. "He broke the neck of a pullet and took it away with him, and the eggs as well. He snickered and pushed me against the wall with his hands. They're robbers!"

"They're murderers," said Callum and lit a splinter of wood from the fire.

"They're sleeping in my own bed," said another woman. "They've thrown sand on the floor where they shot my boy, because I couldn't scrub away the blood."

There was an uncomfortable silence until the old man said again. "Yon's daft behaviour! We're not the military."

"Is it true?" said another man fiercely, "Have there been landings, Callum?"

"We don't know," said Callum, "We canna listen to the wireless now. We shall only know what they care to tell us."

"*What are we going to do?*"

Some one had kicked over a tea-cup, but no one noticed it, and the brown stream ran across the floor-stones and eddied about the toe of Callum's boot. He pushed the white ash of tobacco down into his pipe and lit it again.

"What can you do against yon guns? We know nothing about guns, and they've our boats."

Callum looked at the speaker closely. "By morning," he said, as if deliberating each word with himself, "the boats will have gone. They won't let us pull them up and the storm is rising along the Gutter."

They cried out in pain: "Our boats!"

Callum took his pipe from his teeth and said quickly and a little scornfully, "Oh, aye, 'Our boats'! But don't you see if the boats go then they canna use them either? They'll never get away."

"But they're *our* boats!"

"And they've still got guns," said the woman whose son had been killed,

"Aye," said Callum. "They have guns."

"*What are we going to do?*"

Callum's pipe had gone out again. He lit another splinter and the flame jumped up and down above the bowl. It singed his eyebrows and the islanders could smell the burnt hair. He smiled guiltily and rubbed the back of his hand across his brows. "I don't know. We must wait. We must wait and do nothing for them, I know. There's blood on their hands. They killed a man and a dog, they've probably killed others elsewhere. But if we do nothing, then we shall be strong too."

"What did they say to you?" asked the man with the stick. "Callum man, tell us. You've been over there talking to yon. What did they say to you?"

"They said they were strong, too. Aye, they laughed at us and said everything would be fine if we held our tongues."

"We canna know," said a woman sadly, "Perhaps they're right, they have landed across the water."

And the old man added: "If that's true, shall we not do as they ask? It's enough with the storm and the young folk away at the war. They'll be back soon, now that it's over. We canna do anything, and they'll only make it harder for us when the others come from the mainland. . . ."

A woman shouted sharply, "They canna shoot us all! They dinna want this island!"

"But they'll let our boats be destroyed."

"No one has asked them. . . ."

"It's no good," said Callum. "They don't trust us, man!"

"But if we promised. . . ."

"They don't trust us!" said Callum angrily. "Don't you see why? Everywhere they go they do these things. They come and take away men's lives and destroy their property. Aye, and in some places men turn on them and are murdered. So yon fellows can trust none but themselves."

"Callum," said his wife gently. "You angered them."

"Woman, have you forgotten the boy?" he said in amazement. "I don't know what we should do, except wait. Aye, we'll wait. If God does not destroy our boats in the storm, we must ourselves. I *know* we must do that, because yon men must not get away. Perhaps what they say about the mainland is lies, but we must do nothing for them. Nothing!"

He looked at the people in the little room, his wife standing by her brother looking at him strangely, his niece and her child. He knew them well. He knew their boats, and what vegetables they had planted among the stones in the black earth behind their homes. With them, in the rain, he had hauled up their boats out of reach of December storms. And with their wives he had stood on the ruined jetty and waited for them to come in from the sea. He had led them at prayers, taken their sons across to the mainland to serve in the warships; stood by the graves on the braeside with the wind on his bared head when one of them died.

He felt tired.

His wife came up and took his arm. "We canna do anything, Callum man," she said softly. "But we'll wait because you say so." And she asked that they should sing another psalm.

So they sang, all but the old man, who thumped on the floor in exasperation, all out of time and fitfully.

"*Behold how good and pleasant it is for brethren to dwell together in unity. . . .*"

"We must wait!" said Callum obstinately when they had sung.

One of the babies began to cry. It bent its body backward and pushed at its mother with feet and fists, it closed its mouth and opened it again. It began to splutter and all the women there turned their attention to it with relief. Callum felt as if something had suddenly come between him and this life, and he did not know what it was. "We must wait," he said again. "We don't know these people, and we don't know what they might do."

The old man said, "If what they said is true, perhaps it would be wiser . . ." and, without finishing, he hid his confusion by leaning forward, poking for the medallion with his stick. "What was yon toy they gave the bairns?"

The baby was quiet for a while, and then began to whimper again, pushing against its mother and stuffing its tiny fists against its head. Outside the storm blustered and drew itself up, then, for a moment, as if in exhaustion, the noise subsided. The air was quiet. The islanders listened, for outside they had heard someone whistling one of their own melodies.

Then the wind brought in the rain again. Callum tapped out his pipe, he did not want to smoke. He too felt relieved, for there was something outside that he did understand. The storm. He knew what that would do.

THEY STAY

I

THE pilot was shaving by the window. He had a little hot water in a thick mug that had the portraits of King Edward and Queen Alexandra on one side, and a thick gold line about the rim. It gave him some satisfaction to shave out of it.

It was still raining, and the sky was dark, so dark that he could hardly see in the room, but the woman had said there was no more oil for the lamp, and the pilot had become angry then, hammered on the table with his fist and shouted invective at her in a language she did not understand. It was the second time she told him that he could not have what he wanted. The first time was when she said there was no sugar for the tea. He liked sugar and could not drink tea without it, and he thought that there should be plenty on the island.

Eventually Hart had had to boil the shaving water for him, because after the pilot had hit the woman she had locked herself away, and he was too conscious of his dignity to break down the door.

Although he was still very angry, he was quite calm now, and he was shaving carefully. He was altogether very careful about his appearance, and that morning Hart had pressed his uniform. He held his face close to the mirror, pulling taut the pink skin with his fingers and pressing the razor against it. The rain rattled against the window and he looked at it and swore softly. He felt himself growing bored with the island already. Three days ago, when they came down the hillside, he had been excited by the conquest. Now it was successful he was bored. He ran his finger thoughtfully across his upper lip and toyed with the idea of growing a moustache. He dismissed it as affectation. The islanders were quiet. Since the night the storm had destroyed three of their boats and damaged the fourth, they had been sullen, he thought. They hardly put in an appearance. One or two of them would work in their gardens, but when he came out on the jetty they went inside and closed the doors.

Still, he wasn't to be fooled, and the gun stood always at the door. Its arc of fire covered each cottage, and the hill face. Once Hart had opened fire, a short burst. There were children screaming and the lieutenant had gone outside. Hart said that two children had tried to go up the hill, and then the old fool who said he was the leader came and protested. He stood before the pilot carelessly, with his hands in his pockets across his belly, and said something or other that Mann couldn't translate. But the pilot abused the islander and sent him away.

Perhaps he should have been harsher, but there had been no trouble after that, and the pilot grew bored. Mann said the islanders wouldn't talk to him; they were angry about their boats, he said.

Mann. . . . The pilot passed the razor gently down the cleft in his chin. It was always difficult to shave there. That one physical feature he had inherited from his mother was a nuisance. Mann was a strange fellow; it was lucky he was a good navigator.

He lathered his face again. The soap was pink and smelt strongly of antiseptic. In France there was scented toilet soap. Mann was a good navigator, but it was only his second flight with the pilot and they did not know each other. Hart was different, they had been flying for months, and they knew what each required of the other. It was a pity Hart did not have Mann's intelligence. So long as Mann obeyed orders it was all right.

As he passed the razor over the cleft in his chin the pilot thought of his mother again. She had been a pretty woman, but the cleft in her chin spoilt her lips, and made them appear coarse. Her father had been a butcher. He owned a chain of shops in the northern towns, and an abattoir outside Bremen. She had been married when the last war began, to a man who had earned the pilot's delayed respect by getting killed in the war. The pilot remembered his grandfather. He was very thin, with a tuft of hairs protruding from each ear, a high starched collar, and a guttural manner of slurring his "r's" that the pilot had always found irritating. But he had given money to Hitler. The pilot thought of Hitler at Nuremberg, and the flags, and the shouts of "*Sieg Heil!*" As he wiped his face, he looked at the medal ribbon on his tunic where it hung across a chair.

He rolled down his sleeves over his forearms, admiring the muscles there. Mann said once that he had worked in a butcher's shop. It was three days ago when they buried the body of Stern. . . . Stern was an ugly sight, the fighter's cannon had hit him. Mann had said then that when he was a boy he had carried the pails of pigs' and rabbits' blood and poured them down the drains at the back of his father's shop. It was an odd thing to have mentioned then. The pilot thought of Mann's thin black hair and sallow face. He wondered if Mann had Jewish blood, and hadn't the *Protocols of Zion* something to do with a blood ritual?

The Falangists had shot some Jews when he was at Burgos. But they were Communists too. How much of what they said about the Jews was true? It didn't really matter.

Stern had been an ugly sight. The blood had washed right over the control panel, and shone there. The pilot felt the feeling of sickness come over him again as he remembered it, and he realised that he hadn't quite got over the crash. The cannon could quite easily have hit him. It was just as well it didn't, for Stern would have bungled this job. It had been a good idea to sit there on the stone, to smoke, and get a grip of one's self. A good idea to grapple with a new problem before the crash had time to get the better of him. No good being nervous, that was a weakness. But Stern had been an ugly sight, an unclean thing to be spattered over the plane. The pilot had seen it all quite plainly even afterwards when he had been sitting on the stone in the rain. You couldn't sleep with that in your mind, and he thought contemptuously of the N.C.Os. asleep beneath the tarpaulin. Hart actually snored. They were insensitive, stupidly so.

But would he be able to fly again, that was it? Had his nerve gone? He'd never know until he took the plane up again. Not that plane, another, and another, and another. It wasn't the first crash, there had been others, but they had been in sunlight, with his machine getting smaller and smaller beneath him as he drifted down below the cupola of his parachute. And he had gone up again immediately he landed. But not this time; he had come down in the dark, with Stern's broken body falling across him, and Hell knows what speeding up toward him in the darkness.

But that was the best of it, don't you see? Although you didn't

know what was to happen, you've triumphed just the same. Be
sensitive about things, but don't be nervous, and plan, always
plan. Yet he felt sick still; it must be the smell of the soap.

The pilot resented the smell of the antiseptic soap. The woman
had looked queer when she gave it to him, with a twist of her
lips as if she were enjoying some joke. All these islanders had cold
faces, as if they had been chipped from the rocks. He felt in his
tunic pocket for a cigarette, and lit it so that the smoke might
kill the smell.

He sat in the chair and crossed his legs, thoughtfully, and with
the toe of one boot he began to kick at the bulbous leg of the table.
Three days. Nothing yet. What had the radio said?

"Large squadrons of our air forces attacked the enemy's bases
this morning. . . . Fires were observed. One fighter shot
down. . . ."

Nothing more. It wasn't easy to wait, he wasn't used to it.
Perhaps they could take the other boat and make their way to
the mainland if nothing happened. That fellow with the tarred
hands had shaken his head about the boat. The lieutenant bit
his lips with anger. The destruction of the boats had been
maliciously desired by the islanders. It was sabotage.

He took out his log-book and filled it in:

"Third day: Storm still on. Korporal Mann reports islanders
as stating that it will get worse. Little rain. High seas have destroyed three of the four boats, fourth badly damaged. Stones of
the jetty being carried away. No important radio news. Islanders
quiet. Suspect trouble. Preparations made. . . ."

Preparations made . . . yes. He wished he could speak English.
He didn't like relying on Mann all the time. Did the fellow have
Jewish blood? The lieutenant suddenly realised how much he
detested the navigator's sallow skin. "We must build a nation of
strong, blonde, Aryan heroes!" That was what Streicher had said
at Nuremberg. The pilot laughed shortly. Streicher was bald and
fat, but he might have been talking about Hart.

What could the islanders do? They didn't know how to fight,
they were only old men, except the boy, and the pilot had seen
him playing with a small boat. He had killed the other young
man. There might have been more, but they were probably at

sea. It might have been different had there been more young men. The lieutenant put himself in their place, it was a good exercise. A swift rush at the cottage, quite easily they could do that, even though some would be killed. But he had told Mann to tell them that if they did that the second gun on the jetty would fire into the cottages where the women were.

The wind dipped and blew the smoke into the room, until the pilot coughed and stared at the fire angrily. He looked at his notebook. It contained the log of the plane's flight and the laconic entry: "Leutnant Stern killed by cannon fire."

Stern had spoken English. He had had a flask of brandy in his pocket, and they must have buried it with him, which was a pity. Stern had been a big man, with a red face and eyebrows like Hart's, so fair that you could hardly see them. Streicher would have liked him too. He wore pince-nez when he thought no one was looking. He was always humming student songs, and he said that the scar on his face had been won in a duel. He called the lieutenant a "pork-butcher's suckling", but that was only when he was drunk, and the lieutenant paid no attention to him or anyone else when they were drunk. Besides he had been a good pilot. He had flown a dive-bomber over the Polish fort at Danzig and taken films of it.

Now he was dead, and he had spoken English.

The lieutenant did not suppose that the islanders drank at all.

Hart was a womaniser. Was there a pretty woman on the island, behind these big skirts and black stockings, behind these red faces and big calloused hands? Hart would find her, but that would cause trouble. Hart must be warned.

He stood up and pulled at his tunic, and fastened the buttons beneath his chin. He smoothed out the medal ribbon and straightened his pilot's badge. His cap was getting dirty, and there was no polish for his boots. He rubbed at them with the edge of the table-cloth. He would go and see the men at the guns. He bent down and looked through the window. There was a geranium on the sill and as he pushed the leaves aside a bloom broke off and fell to the floor. He trod on it.

The storm wept against the window, and he could hardly see. The glass was crude, and, with the rain streams, aborted the view of the other cottages. The door of one was open. A child in a blue dress stood there and the wind blew her hair back from her face and the dress about her figure. She held the arm of a wooden doll and it dangled by her side. Then someone grasped her and pulled her inside. The door closed, and shone a little with the rain on it.

The lieutenant smiled and straightened his body.

By the time he left the room the bitter scent of the crushed flower was quite strong.

II

HART knew that the woman lived alone. During the time he had sat by the gun in the doorway hers had been the cottage he watched most conscientiously. It stood at the end of the row, there always seemed to be washing hanging from the line, as soon as the rain dropped a little, and when it came on again she would gather it in. It amused Hart to see her clutching a great armful of clothes, and he whistled at her mockingly.

She had two children, a boy and a girl who played in the open doorway, and stared at the airman with their fingers in their mouths. Sometimes they would come outside and then the woman would appear again and take them inside, looking across at Hart and pushing back her hair with one hand. But the woman was young. She was pretty in a way that Hart considered crude but desirable, and the sight of her with her arms bare above the elbow stirred him. When he saw her watching him as he sat behind the gun he smiled and flicked a cigarette towards her. But the gesture went unanswered, and when the door closed behind her Hart felt the fury that raged suddenly inside him. Hart thought of her bare arms, and he thought of what the pilot had told him about the woman, and he scratched his thigh irritably. He lolled now against the wall of the cottage, scraping the white flakes with his shoulders, and feeling in his tunic for another cigarette.

Behind him, along the stretch of beach, the sea rolled in

magnificently and crashed on the stones. The waves were very high, they rode over the jetty and drained themselves from it in yellow foam. Far, far out their heads were white, and occasionally the heavy clouds bit them with rain. Hart hated the weather. Rain, and the ceaseless beat of the wind. He was never sluggish and idleness stirred him into impatience. He smoked heavily and thought of the woman behind the windows of the cottage. He thought of going across there at night, when the darkness was thickest, when the rain was coming down the slope, when the silence from the pilot's room meant that he was asleep at last. He thought of going across there at night when Mann was on the jetty with the other gun and Grun lay moaning to himself in the corner of the room behind. He thought of going across there at night when she was in her bed and alone.

But he dared not leave the gun, and he trusted the pilot. So when he was on guard he sat there snapping open the bolt, refeeding the belt. Smoking, smoking, and thinking of the woman. He forgot the war then, and did not realise why he sat there in the dark, because he thought of the woman across the pebbles. He forgot the "*Horst Wessel*" and the uniform, the seat in the rear of the plane, the songs and the torches and the drinking. He forgot the streets with the red, white and black swastika scars, and he forgot how his heart pumped as he marched. He forgot because he remembered what it was to find a woman, and it had been so long.

But now it was day, if this leaden, blinding, rain-dragged semi-darkness was day, and he was not chained to the gun or to the thought of the pilot. He took shelter from the rain in the open doorway beside Grun, and he narrowed his eyes and looked across to her cottage as he smoked.

She had not sung since the day they came. She had not sung the song that had first attracted his attention. But when the rain stopped a little and the wind rose and blew down from the cliff she would come out of the cottage and hang her washing on the line, and her arms would be round above the elbow. But she never looked at him, and he was angry. He hated her.

Grun was watching him; Hart knew that. He hated the way Grun watched everybody, deciding whether they were doing right or wrong. He hated the thought that perhaps Grun was praying for him. He took the cigarette from his mouth and looked sideways at the man who sat at the gun. Grun was watching him. He had a wide face with dirty skin, and in profile it looked like a half-moon, with chin and forehead receding, nose curving. He looked ascetic. Hart sneered at him as the "Cardinal," and Hart thought he was always praying for somebody.

Hart looked at the sloping profile with distaste. Grun was always worrying. He worried about the islanders, he worried about Mann, he worried about the gun between his knees. Most of all, he worried about Rotterdam. If Grun worried about Rotterdam, he shouldn't have been there.

Grun said: "You stand in the doorway looking over there all the time. What're you after?"

"Mind your own business!"

The wireless operator fingered the belt of the gun. "I shouldn't think you'd worry about women at a time like this."

"At a time like this! And I don't worry about women, I want them to worry about me!" Hart hated the chanting, snivelling way Grun put everything. He felt in his pockets for the cigarettes he knew were not there. He had smoked the last, but he would not ask Grun for one. He would not ask favours. He bent down and laughed in the operator's face.

"Have you never had a woman, or do you want her too?"

"I don't want to quarrel with you."

Hart spat into the rain and thrust his hands in his pockets. "You want nothing. What made you become an airman?" Grun did not answer.

He could not go across now. He had been thinking of going across. The thought of going across there, opening the door and finding her alone in the house made him weak, and turned his inside to water. The small of his back ached. And now he could not do it because Grun was watching. But the power of being able to do so did he choose was intoxicating. Nothing stood in his way but Grun there, with his weak chin and dark eyes. He could hardly see, the blood seemed to flood his vision.

But Grun was there watching him, and to go across now would seem weak. He cursed Grun and thought of how he hated the woman, her round arms, her big breasts, and the washing she hung on the line. The craving for a cigarette was too strong. He turned to Grun. The operator was looking out across the rain to the cottages, his hands folded across the breach of the gun. It was getting near dusk and his face looked more sallow as the shadows crept into the pocked skin. He sat quite still and jumped when Hart said:

"Give me a cigarette."

"You have your own."

"If I had any, do you think I'd beg from you? Give me one."

Grun handed up the packet and Hart took it distastefully. "These are foul."

"You needn't smoke them if you don't want to."

Hart stopped in the motion of putting the cigarette between his lips. He looked at the wireless operator suspiciously. "You've been drinking."

"I haven't."

"You had none of your own, I know that. But you've been drinking just the same."

"What of it? Do you want to 'beg' for that too?"

Hart flung the cigarettes at him angrily. "Where did you get it, that's what I want to know?" He stopped in the action of lighting the cigarette, "*Stern!*"

Grun looked away, but Hart went on hurriedly, "Stern carried a flask in his pocket. He used to give me some when he was drunk. You took it out of there when we buried him. You dirty scavenger. Stealing from a dead hero!"

Grun laughed; it was like a little scream. "You don't have to talk that nonsense to me. Dead murderers, that's all we're ever likely to be!"

Hart hit him in the face with a clenched fist and Grun staggered back across the gun. He quivered, looked as if he were about to cry, and he sucked at the blood on his lips. Hart's arm was drawn back, ready to hit again. His eyes shone and he was angry.

Grun sat down at the gun again and dabbed at his mouth with the back of his hand. "It was my brandy," he said. "It was mine."

"You're a liar!" shouted Hart. "You always were, you lying bastard!"

"You want to fight me," said Grun. "You want to fight everybody. But not me. The lieutenant told me to sit here with the gun, so I'm not going to fight you, so go on insulting if you think it's worth the waste of breath."

Hart flung the cigarette at him and it jolted from Grun's shoulder with a burst of sparks. He thrust his hands in his pocket.

"You stole brandy out of a dead man's pocket."

"It was my brandy," said Grun again. "I've told you it was mine."

Hart said nothing, and for a while both stared at the weather. "Give me some," said Hart finally, and Grun handed him the flask. Hart wiped his mouth with appreciation.

"That was good," he said. "Stern must have got it from Paris."

"Will we ever get back there again?"

"Of course. We've got to wait, and the boy'll see us through." He looked at the brandy and again clicked his lips.

Grun's lips were still bleeding. He wiped them with a handkerchief and looked at the stains as he said: "I don't like these people. And nothing happens. They look at me as I sit here, they look out of their windows and I know they are hating me and would kill me perhaps if I weren't behind this gun."

Hart grinned. "It's the gun. See what it can do? Because we've these guns they daren't touch us. There are more guns and we can use them. We're pretty powerful, and people like this are a miserable lot.

"I know," said Grun. He sounded tired. "But I don't like being watched all the time, being hated by people who look at me from behind their curtains and never invite me in. I'd like them to talk to me, you know, Hart. I used to think it would be different, that they'd welcome us with flowers, as we were told they would. But everywhere we go they seem to hate us and we kill them because we are hated."

"They're jealous of us, you idiot!" He laughed. "And I don't want them to love me, except the women."

Grun went on talking as if he had not heard Hart. "And yet,

if we hadn't killed that man it might have been different."

Hart bent forward and shouted at him angrily.

"You've been talking to Mann!"

"If you're going to hit me . . ."

"I'm not going to hit you, you snivelling old woman. But Mann's a liar. His grandmother was a Jewess!"

"You hate him, and are just trying to slander him."

"You can't help but recognise these Jews."

Grun looked at him shrewdly. "It's got you too, this waiting, and having people watch you, and only me to talk to. You only talk to me because Mann won't listen to you, and the lieutenant doesn't trust you."

Hart grabbed him by the tunic and shook him. "You're a liar, a canting, superstitious liar! Because your stomach turned over in your mouth at Rotterdam, you think you can sit and moralise about men who haven't got milk and water for their guts!"

Grun dragged himself free. He was pale and his hands shook as he buttoned his tunic.

"You want to fight me. Go and get your woman. It's always the same, when you want a woman and can't get one you have to do something violent. I think you joined the Party because of that. Now hit me again."

Hart pulled at his sleeves. "I'm not going to hit you again," he said. "But I'll tell the lieutenant you're a danger to us all. Even Mann is better than you."

Grun paused. "You needn't tell him," he said. "I was angry, that's all, but you brought it on yourself." His voice rose a little. "It's sitting here waiting, and nothing happening." He looked at Hart slyly. "Haven't you thought it queer that that woman should keep hanging her washing out."

"What do you mean?" Hart found he wanted to talk about her.

"Well, there's a storm on and yet she still hangs out her washing. If a plane went over they'd see the washing and think it queer too, and may be send somebody to see what was up. Do you think she's signalling?"

Hart snorted and kicked at the earth with his boot. Grun had been right. When he wanted a woman he fought. In Spain. In Poland, in France, and now here. He wanted to fight Grun, he wanted to fight these islanders because they sat behind their curtains and because across the rough ground there was a woman.

"There might be something in it, though," he said, and he took his hands out of his pocket. "I'm going along the beach. Perhaps I'll go over there and see what she's up to." He walked off, with his head bent against the wind.

Grun watched him go and smiled contemptuously. He'll go across to the cottage; when he thinks I'm not watching he'll go across, and if he's lucky in what he finds he'll come back and play cards with me and laugh, and we'll be friends for a while. I'm thirsty, there's more brandy, but some of it must be saved.

Before Rotterdam there had been no drinking, but afterwards it had been essential, because, if not, there was always the vision of blossoming bombs, and people running, and whole blocks of building crumbling like sand before a tide. And those things got between the sights of a gun and an enemy fighter, and between you and God when you prayed. A little drink helped. The flask was of silver, and Stern's initials were engraved within laurel leaves.

Pater noster, qui es in coelis, sanctificetur nomen tuum. . . .

Perhaps down there had been long white candles, and boys singing, and the light through blood-red glass. There hadn't been people bleeding so far as he could see from the turret, but they had run in the street, here and there, with no apparent purpose, and buildings had fallen upon them. And he watched it for an hour.

Ave Maria, gratia plena. Dominus tecum, benedicta tu. . . .

Before Rotterdam. . . . Before Rotterdam there should have been a crash. He had thought that when he heard the cannon shells hitting the fuselage and felt the machine shuddering horribly. He thought that then, but not for long because fear swamped over him and drowned everything else. He had screamed, opening his mouth until the lips were drawn so tight that the skin split. He had strained his lungs so with the scream that no sound came eventually, and the incline of the plane had rolled him away from the gun down towards Mann. Then there had been the smell of the oil, of blood, and someone shouting that Stern had been killed. He remembered clutching at the stays and shouting to the Holy Mother that he didn't want to die, and thinking that if he had to die, why hadn't it been before Rotterdam?

And Mann, even as the plane went down, was asking him why he hadn't fired the gun. He hadn't fired because the rain stained his vision, outside there was darkness. Once he had seen tracers coming from the fighter. But he hadn't fired. And then the plane went down, and the screaming of the wind went through the fuselage, and he didn't know whether it was he or the wind making the noise as he lay on the floor of the plane.

He remembered it all and he sat trembling at the gun, wanting to vomit all over again with the memory of it.

The lieutenant had killed the dog by hitting it on the head, and after they had gone down Grun had laid beside the carcass, watching them go down to the cottages. And soon the children had climbed up to him, to cry when they saw the dog and entangle their fingers in its thick hair, and the boy had bitten angrily at his fist. They did not seem to like the medallion with the Mother of Christ's head on it. The girl's dark hair had been in plaits and her eyes were black, her skin brown. There were spring flowers in the design of her cotton frock and she twisted the pleats of the skirt between her fingers. She wore boy's boots with mud in the seams. And when he opened fire at the chimney they both ran away and left him beside the dead dog. He gave them the medallion because they had cried about the dog, and stroked its hair. The girl had refused it, but the boy took it with his eyes on the gun and one fist in his mouth. The dog's head looked queer because the blow had been heavy.

It was Stern's brandy, but he hadn't taken it out of the officer's pocket at the time they buried him. They hadn't buried him very deep. There were great boulders in the earth and it was night, and only the broken fuselage to dig with. It had been easy to dig the body up again before he went down with the gun, and he had tried not to think it was horrible. Some photographs had fallen out of the pocket. You could buy them in Paris, Hart had some, and there was one of a woman Grun imagined to be the dead man's sister. He couldn't see very well.

Perhaps he would send the flask to her when the brandy was

gone. He had kept the photograph; it had an address on the back.

It became dark quickly. He could hardly see the cottage now. When it was night Hart would come back and try to get into the cottage without being seen. The islanders would light their lamps and he would have to shout, and perhaps fire a round to make them put up their curtains. And the storm would get worse at night, under cover of the darkness it would encroach on the island and tear away more of the jetty. It had been very bad the night the boats were destroyed, when the leader of the islanders had come to the door of his cottage and stood there in the open, with his hands in his pockets across his belly, watching the timbers being torn from the hulls and dragged out by the waves. Grun knew he should have fired at the man, but he let him stand there until he went in.

. . . *Fiat voluntas tua, sicut in coelo*. . . .

Soon they would come, and there would be medals perhaps, and the worry and anxiety, the soul-torturing anxiety, would be over and he would share in the greatness and not have to endure the pangs that gave birth to it. For Hart it was easy, for Mann it was a mystery perhaps, for the officer it meant planning, constant activity. Not sitting behind a gun, or giving medallions to small children because a dog had been killed.

The storm was high now. The waves roared over the stones, and the rain began to fall more heavily. Over the cliff top the darkness was thick and rolled down on the white cottages.

Panem nostrum quotidianum da nobis hodie. . . .

Hart went along the beach. He did not pass Mann, who sat on the jetty by the wreckage of what was left of the last boat. He went the other way, where the beach gave way to black rocks and the rising of the island. He did not walk for pleasure. When the darkness came he would turn away and go to the cottage and find the woman. He hated the island and the storm. He hated waiting, but he caught the pilot's enthusiasm for success and power, so that he exulted in a way that the weakling Grun and the doubter Mann could never do. He turned up his coat collar and withdrew his short neck and head into it, hunching his shoulders and thrusting his hands into his pockets. He climbed up away from the beach, for the wind was pushing in a wall of spray that had already drenched his thin tunic. He sat by a rock, crouched on his haunches, and waited for complete darkness.

It came quickly, as if the wind, in a moment of great strength, had summoned up night and enveloped the island in it. It was hard to find the way back. He climbed the hill so that he might come upon the cottage from the rear, and he stumbled in the holes and across the low walls. He was trembling and his face was hot. As he passed the cottages he could hear voices, a child crying, and from one, some singing. There were vegetables and coarse flowers in the gardens, in one a pig-sty where the pigs squealed and snorted when he dropped in among them. He kicked at them until they turned on him, and then he leaped over the wall and went on.

When he reached the cottage there was no light, and the door at the back was banging open.

In the room the fire was dying, and there was the hot smell of ironed clothes, draped across the broad back of a chair before it. The room was empty, and he stood silently at the doorway. He heard children's voices whispering above, and once, when his boots scraped on the floor-stones, they called out a question. But soon, as he stood there until the acrid smell of his own damp clothes and mired boots overcame the smell of the room, they were quiet.

He lit a match, shaded it until he could see the lamp on the table, and then he lit that too. He looked about the room. A woman's dress, freshly-ironed, hung by the fire, and the sight of it stirred his blood and the saliva in his mouth. There were cups on the table and brass dishes above the fire. A child's book lay on the seat of a severe arm-chair and he picked it up and flicked over its pages contemptuously. At an illustration of a boy in a paper cap, with a wooden sword, he grinned, and threw the book on the fire. The flames danced up from its curling leaves and he held his hands over them and shivered. Against the dark curtains at the little window the flowers of a geranium glowed dully.

He left the fire to close the door and then he sat by the fire, and poked it until it glowed. The draught sucked the scraps of the burnt book up the chimney. It was hard to wait and he rubbed his hands and wondered why he was quivering so much.

It was not usually like this.

But it was not long to wait. He heard steps outside, and before he could get up the woman came in. She closed the door, and because she was locking it she did not see him until she turned, and then she leant against the door with her hands behind her back, looking at him.

Hart stood up, and she pushed at her hair nervously with both hands. She glanced to the stairs. Hart tried to grin, but he was out of breath and his hands were twitching uncontrollably. The woman looked at him and her mouth was open. A shawl fell from her shoulders and he looked at her bare arms.

He looked at her and held his breath.

She didn't scream, and that, more than anything throughout what followed, surprised him most. He wondered, though, why she kept her eyes fixed on the stairway, and why she seemed to be listening for something, even when she struggled.

III

BESIDE the other gun on the jetty sat Mann. He and Hart had erected an emplacement of stones and stretched a tarpaulin across it, but, despite that, the wind found entry and with it the rain and the sea-spray. Mann sat there quite silently; he was not a man given to much movement and he liked to watch the island wrestling with the storm. Like a wedge of wood, it rode the surface of the sea and thrust itself against the wind. For reasons he could not explain to himself, Mann found admiration for the strength of this island, and with it went a regard for the stoutness of the islanders' cottages and their low flake walls.

The beach sloped away from him on either side, and rolled and moved continuously with the sucking drag of the waves. Fifteen feet behind him the fall of the sea over the broken jetty ended, and regularly every few seconds he heard the rising sound of a breaker coming in, until it crashed on the stones and broke there. He felt the water hitting the tarpaulin. It was not a safe spot to place the gun, but the only one tactically. It covered the other gun and the cottage, and to his right the last boat which had now been drawn out of reach of the sea and lay with its mast broken, its hull holed, and the sail draped over it carelessly. There were numerals in white on the bows, and a woman's name. By a coincidence that Mann regarded a little wryly, it was his wife's name.

He had been there for some time: the men spent long periods at the guns. During the intervals Mann slept profoundly, as did Grun. Hart, he knew, spent his time wandering about the beaches. A few moments ago he had seen him slouch away from the cottage and go up toward the mass of black stones that buttressed the island against the sea to the south. He did not know yet whether evening had come. It had been dark all the afternoon and the rain incessant, and the sky to the west was still black. Mann's mouth was dry with salt and his hands cold. Occasionally he would cup them about a cigarette, partly to warm them, but mostly to hide the ember from the eyes of the lieutenant. He had begun to husband his cigarettes. Smoking was all there was to do, and he did not want to exhaust what few he had left. He inhaled deeply and felt the burning smoke in his lungs.

He saw the woman come out of the cottage. He could see her quite plainly from where he sat, and he wondered why Grun, at the cottage door, did not notice her too. She left by the back, and he saw her climbing the wall, bent forward against the wind and holding her shawl over her head. He looked at her curiously, but prepared his gun. He trained it on her to follow her movements. She kept looking toward his shelter, but seemed to think that he could not see her, for she took clumsy shelter behind the walls and clumps. He watched her carefully, suspiciously, as she made her way along the slope of the hill until the boat obscured her from his view, and then he did not see her again for some minutes.

He grew alarmed; he stood up and left the gun shelter. He thought of shouting, but realised that that would arouse the lieutenant. He should not have let the woman get that far, he should have fired, but these were things he *should* have done, and he did not know what to do now. He sat down at the gun and aimed it at the boat, and waited.

He saw her again. He saw her head looking at him from the stern of the vessel, then it was withdrawn, and this went on for some minutes. He realised that she was frightened, and this relieved him. He waited for something to happen and felt the same nervous anticipation that often attended him in the plane.

She came out from behind the boat at last and began to walk resolutely across the pebbles toward him. She stumbled and slipped inelegantly and the wind moulded the skirt about her legs. About five yards from him she stopped. Mann rattled the breech of the gun and she stepped back and looked up at him.

"What do you want?" he asked.

She had not understood him, but inclined her head forward, still listening. She poked at strands of her hair and pushed them beneath a shawl. He repeated the question.

"You're the one who brought the boy's body across?" she said.

For the moment Mann did not understand her, then he remembered. The boy the lieutenant had killed. Neither Grun nor Hart had shown an interest in the body, and Mann had carried it across his shoulder to the cottages. He remembered they had placed it on a sofa and covered it with a table-cloth and the leader had thanked him. He did not remember the woman.

He said "Yes," and then added, "Why?"

She did not answer the question, but asked in return, "Can you understand what I'm saying?"

"It's not easy," he said. "You sound as if you were singing. I've never heard English spoken like this. Are you English?"

"It's not our language," she said, answering the question with impatience, but as if reluctant to say what she wanted. "Most of us have forgotten the old language."

"What do you want?" said Mann suspiciously, and the woman stepped forward. The pebbles slipped beneath her feet and she staggered against the wind. Mann was alarmed, he did not know what she might do.

"Stay where you are!"

"I want to talk to you."

"There's nothing to talk about. You must see the lieutenant."

"It wouldn't interest him."

"I'm on guard here," said Mann. "I can't talk to you. You

should .have remained in your house. I should have shot you."

"You should have shot me," she repeated. " Is that all, man?"

"They're my orders. We can't trust you."

"You don't know us; why should you shoot us?"

"We're at war."

She stared at him from below the jetty and he did not like the look. "Go back to your house," he said roughly.

"I've come to talk to you."

"Go back to your house. If there's anything you want to ask you must tell your leader to see the lieutenant."

"You don't understand."

"It doesn't matter; you must go back to your house."

It was getting darker, but he could see her clearly. She stood below him on the beach, her body foreshortened and her head lifted so that she could see him. A thick shawl was across her head and shoulders, but the wind had tugged loose the hair. It's fair, Mann thought, she looks like a German woman. She was young and largely built, her face was round, and he liked the high forehead. The lips were full and the eyes blue, and a slight frown gave character to a face that was otherwise placid. Her legs were strong and her hands coarse, but he liked her voice, it *was* as if she were singing.

"Please go back to your house," he said.

"There are things I must ask you, things we want to know, but you're making it hard to say them."

"You must ask the lieutenant, he . . ."

"We don't want to speak to him. He'll do nothing for us."

"Nor will I."

"You're hard." She looked at him closely, with her head held up and the chin forward.

"Who sent you here?" asked Mann abruptly.

"No one."

"Then there's nothing to be done. Please go back, or I must call the lieutenant."

"You won't do that, you'll be blamed for not shooting me."

Mann thought she smiled then, and he replied angrily, "You don't understand what I must do."

She looked at him again and pushed the wet hair from her forehead, the frown had deepened. "You're right, we don't understand you, we don't understand what you do."

Mann smiled this time, he felt sure of himself. "It's because you're so weak."

She looked at him critically, at his legs, his narrow chest and hollow face. There was a note of contempt in her voice. "Och! you're not strong. My husband and my father are larger men than you. They fish alone, and that takes strength."

"It's power I meant," and he looked at the gun between them.

"Aye, you have guns, and you've killed a man and a dog since you came here. You've robbed us and bullied us, and for all this you gave us a little piece of metal with a woman's head on it."

Mann did not understand her. "We need the guns. . . ."

"Why?"

"There are things you don't understand, nations that are jealous. These things are beyond you all, you're too simple or too stupid."

"We're not jealous of you, we don't like the way you behave. We don't want to do those things. But . . ."

"But you sent armies against us. . . ."

"You killed a boy here for nothing at all. Perhaps you killed others."

"Is death so important then?"

She did not answer immediately, and in the pause it suddenly occurred to Mann how stupid his question had been. He wiped his hands nervously on his trousers.

She began to speak quickly. "We've lived on this island for a long time. If you go up the brae you'll see our graveyard and the stones there are very old, and some of the names on them are strange to us now. Sometimes there were many of us, sometimes a few like now. Our men go out to fish and sometimes storms like this drown them. And sometimes some of us fall sick and die before the doctor can come out to us. Those things we understand because we are used to them. But one morning you come and you kill a dog, and you kill a man, and you keep us from our boats and don't lift a finger when the storm destroys them. And you tell us not to sing our psalms, and you say you should shoot me because I have come out to this jetty where I played when I was a girl. These things we don't understand." She was breathless.

"You're a woman."

"I'm a man too. I dig with the rest, and I've been out with the boat when there was a steamer on the sands last December. I've two children and while my husband is away I work for them. I've a woman's body, perhaps, but a man's hands." And she held them out to him. They were large and red with so much washing. The nails were broken.

"You're only a girl. You can't understand what's happening."

"I've two bairns and my husband is at sea. On the island we grow up quickly because we must. The fish don't wait for us."

"You don't understand what I mean," said Mann wearily.

"No, we don't understand."

There was another long silence, and again Mann felt foolish, but he liked listening to her. It grew darker, but he could still see her round face and big hands. "You must go," he said at last.

"No," she said firmly. "I want you to ask your officer to let us alone. Let us repair the boat on the shore, so that we can take you to the mainland and give you up to the soldiers."

Mann laughed. "That's funny."

She went on, ignoring his laughter. "Because if you don't the men here will fight you. We live by the sea, and because you have destroyed our boats we canna live. We're not used to being idle."

"We'll allow you to go to sea when our friends come."

"I don't believe you have taken the mainland," she said pathetically.

"We know we have."

She looked about her. "It's our island," she said.

"It's a good island," said Mann approvingly. "If I were a boy I'd like it here. Do your children collect eggs from the nests on the cliffs?"

She looked at him curiously. "Why do you ask that?"

"I'd like to know."

"They're too young," she said. "But I did when I was young."

"You must be brave."

"No, but it's our island, you see."

"It belongs to us now," he said. "What do you call it?"

She told him.

"I don't understand. That's not English, is it?"

"No, it's our own tongue, man. They say it's the tongue the wee folk taught us when we first came."

"What does it mean?"

"The place where the sea breaks."

Mann looked up at the cliff. Occasionally, against the grey sky, a feather of white floated over the top. The sea was striking the cliff face. He nodded his head.

'It *is* our island," she repeated.

"No," he said, and his voice was gentler. "We've taken it. You live here, you and your people live and die here, but your society is decaying, and all over the world, about which you know nothing, there is this decay. Soon, perhaps, there would be no one on this island but the gulls. But now that we've come it'll be different. We're not decaying, we've found strength and power. But it's hard to make you see that."

"Och," she said in disgust. "You're like a bairn saying his lessons!"

"It's what I believe."

"We're not decaying; you talk as if we were daft!"

"You're a woman," he said angrily; "you'll be crying soon."

She grew angry too. "Man, will you be passing laws against that, now?"

"We have no time for it."

"Because you've always won!"

"Because we're strong in spirit."

The shawl had fallen from her head and she gesticulated fiercely. "Spirit, he says! What do you know of spirit, man? Our island has a fine power, so has the sea, aye, and they both have spirit too. But this is the place where the sea breaks!"

"There's no comparison," he said shortly. But he thought of the sea-gulls and the powerful air force they had personified for him. "You're old-fashioned."

"I was wrong to come here," she said.

"I told you to go back, there's nothing you can do. You're a woman, but I can't regard you even as that. You're an enemy."

"Are you married?" she asked quickly.

"Yes," and suddenly he wanted to talk about it. "I have a wife and a boy."

"How old is he?"

"He's six. He'd like this island. I'll tell him all about it, and perhaps I'll bring him here when the war is over."

At home there's nothing but houses, he thought, deep ruts cut in the city. The children played in the streets amid the wheels of traffic, floating tiny boats down the gutters and swinging on the railings. In summer the heat was intense, and although it was a sea-port it was only occasionally that you caught the salty taste of the sea through the dust and smell of garbage from the cellars. Only occasionally could you hear the sound of the ships' sirens above the clang of the electric cars.

And the children's faces were like paper refuse in the alleyways. They marched down the streets behind bands, proud of their brown shirts and black swastikas. . . . Here on the island a child could grow up to love things of which his son knew nothing. After the war, perhaps . . .

"We shan't be glad to see you," she said.

He frowned. "It doesn't matter."

"I'm sorry," she said. "But you could never come as our friend now."

"Why? We're strong." He wanted to plead with her, to tell her about the grey houses and smell of garbage, the children marching in the streets, but what he said was not what he was thinking: "And ruthless perhaps, but it's because we have to be, but to those who are our friends we're generous."

"In the summer," she said, "people would sometimes come out here from the mainland because they liked us and our island. They brought us flowers which we planted in our gardens and sometimes they went fishing with my husband Colin. I liked them because they were good to us, and we understood them." She moved her shawl and plucked at her blouse. "One of them brought me this. It's silk."

Mann smiled. "Well?"

Her voice was bitter now. "But when you came you came down the mountain suddenly. You killed a boy for nothing and you set up guns and let our boats be destroyed. You say you are taking our island from us. We don't want you to be generous. We want you to go!"

Mann's voice was cold. "War is not a matter of silk blouses and flowers from the mainland. Go back to your kitchen, you've no right here."

"*You* have no right here!"

"We're wasting time."

"The sea sets time here. It sets our days and the work we have to do. The sea sets your time too, and perhaps for a long time you'll have to sit at your guns and watch our cottages because you're frightened of us. There are men here and if you won't go when we ask, they'll drive you out." She was crying now.

"You don't understand," said Mann more gently. "Why do you try to?"

"Because it's our island." She looked at him fiercely, he wondered at so calm a face showing so much passion. "You could have come as friends and we would have welcomed you. But you chose to come and kill us, and yet you ask me why I try to understand."

"It's deeper than all this. Please go home to bed."

"You know it's wrong!"

Mann shook his head. "Please go home."

"If you believed all this was right, why didn't you shoot me? It's nothing to kill me. I'm not a woman, you said, I'm an enemy. Yet you would rather gossip to me than kill me."

"Yes," said Mann slowly. "I would like to talk to you. I would like to talk to you because I'm a man and you're a woman. Because I've been away from home a long time, and because it's hard not to get tired of the war. I want to talk to you because I would like this island if I were a boy. But I'm not a boy, and you must go."

"Won't you ask your officer?"

"You must go."

"I'm a woman," she said and struggled with the ideas that flooded her mind. "That means something to you. I've heard about you, you make women your property." She stared at him and said quickly, "If I were to let you make me your property, would you ask your officer?"

Mann stood up, he was very angry, he pushed his hands together.

"Go on back!" he said. "We don't mean anything to you."

"No," she said, and she was calm now. "But if you stay there'll be trouble, and some of our people will be killed."

"Go back!" shouted Mann.

She turned and stumbled up the beach, and then he called to her softly. She stopped, but did not look back.

"What's your name?" he asked.

"It doesn't matter."

"Lock your door," he said. "You'll be safer."

IV

IT was the fifth day and the storm still beat strongly against the island. The lieutenant stood by the door with his crew. He had called in the man from the gun on the jetty because he wished to speak to them all. He looked clean and confident although his boots were unpolished, and because he stood in the shelter of the doorway he seemed more at ease than the crew who stood outside, leaning their heads against the wind and screwing up their eyes when the rain hit them.

"It is over," said the pilot unemotionally. "Our forces have not landed."

There was no reply from the men. They looked at him without a change in their features, as if the unpleasant weather was of more importance, and then Mann glanced involuntarily at the white cottages behind.

"You may smoke," said the lieutenant. But he and Mann only had cigarettes. The lieutenant carefully gave one each to Grun and Hart, and they lit it from one match, cupping their hands about it and bending their heads over it, like men drinking water from their hands.

"You understand what I said," said the lieutenant, slightly surprised by their apparent calm. "We can't expect help from the mainland when this storm stops. How long will it last, Mann?"

"I don't know. Perhaps two more days."

"There's time," said the officer. "We must have that boat patched up, and we will make the people here repair it."

"That will be hard," said Mann.

"It'll be harder for them if they don't. Where do they get their water?"

"From the stream," said Hart. "The women are allowed to go there in the morning." He turned up the collar of his tunic and wished that he could put his hands in his pocket.

The lieutenant exhaled a ring of smoke through the doorway where the wind hungrily seized upon it. "Then they'll draw no more water until we have sufficient volunteers to repair that ship. When it's ready, one of them must accompany us." He looked narrowly at Mann. "What will they say to that?"

Mann thought of the woman. He shrugged his shoulders. "They'd like their boat repaired, of course. Perhaps they'll do it. In fact, I think they'll be glad to get rid of us so easily."

"We shall not leave them with any false impressions," said the pilot casually. "It would be as well to destroy the village before we go. We have been good to these people. Hart!" he said sharply.

"Yes, Herr Leutnant?"

"Have you molested any of them?"

"I haven't spoken to any of them."

"I mean the women, you fool!"

"No, Herr Leutnant."

"Get back to the gun on the jetty." The pilot seemed irritated. Hart winked at Grun as he went off, doubling across the shingle, holding his tunic collar about his neck.

"Mann," said the pilot, "take Grun with you and go through these cottages. Find that insolent fellow and get as many volunteers to repair the boat as possible. Tell them about the water, and make it plain that we mean it."

"Yes, Herr Leutnant. May I ask a question?"

"What is it?"

"Shall I tell them that we are going to the mainland to give ourselves up?"

"What for?" said the pilot harshly.

"They will be more anxious to do it then."

The pilot's face grew pink. "Tell them nothing," he said quickly, "except that it must be done. That's all!"

Mann straightened his cap and took out his pistol. Grun stood up and followed him, and the pilot watched them, still pink in the face and wondering why he felt so irritated. Eventually he went back to the room and wrote in his log:

"Fifth day. Storm still strong. Radio reports indicate that we can expect no help from the mainland. Have instructed Korporal Mann to conscript labour for the repair of the boat. No trouble as yet from the islanders. They are sullen and undemonstrative. Korporal Mann's attitude toward them is not satisfactory."

Then he got up and looked out of the window. Mann was standing at the front door of the first cottage, talking to a woman. As he watched the navigator, he plucked the petals from the last remaining geranium. Grun had turned up his collar too and was hunching his shoulders. He had put his hands in his pockets and seemed indifferent to what was going on. By the woman's skirts was a boy and a girl, and she had an arm about their shoulders.

The pilot returned to the chair by the fire. He looked grave, and he tapped his fingers gently on an empty cigarette case.

Mann did not expect the woman to answer the door when he had rapped on it with his pistol. He knew she lived there, but he did not visualise her opening it. But she pulled it wide with a sweep of her bare arm and the rain began to stain her light blouse almost immediately. The same light frown was on her face. She said nothing, but looked at him as if she had never spoken to him before. Her mouth was loose.

"I must see your husband."

"He isn't here."

"No one was allowed to leave," said Mann in alarm. "You knew that. Where's he gone?"

"He's at sea. . . . I told you that last night. He's been at sea a year." Mann thought that she was smiling slightly, and that the frown disguised it. Two children clung to the thick skirt that hung from her hips, and she put her arms about them suddenly.

"There's no man in this cottage?"

"No."

Mann looked at her closely. He had been wrong when he thought she was smiling, the twist at the corners of her mouth was strained, and her face pale.

"You needn't be frightened," he said, and he put his pistol away. "I'm not going to hurt you." He added this bitterly.

"I'm not afraid of you."

"Where are the men."

"In their own homes, where you keep them. They like your generosity fine!"

"I must ask you not to joke."

"Whatever you *ask*, man, it's still an order."

Mann was angry again. This woman could so easily make him angry. "You make it difficult for us."

"Should I be sorry for that, now?"

"If you and your people were more co-operative, things would be much easier."

"We don't want your co-operation. *It's filthy!* You do nothing when we ask for it, but take everything when you wish, like beasts!"

"I couldn't help you last night, it was a dishonourable suggestion."

She looked at him quietly. "Hasn't he told you then? Hasn't *he*, haven't you both boasted about it?" She was interlocking her fingers at her waist. They were red. "What you were offered as one side of a bargain, you take as your right." She was very excited and the children looked up at her in alarm.

"I don't understand you," said Mann.

"Then ask *him*!"

She closed the door and Mann looked at Grun. "Let's go on," said the wireless operator. "Are we going to stand at all the doors and chat as if it were a market day? What were you talking about?"

"Where did Hart go last night?" asked Mann suspiciously.

"It's not our business."

Mann shrugged his shoulders again. "We'll find this leader. Come on."

Callum opened the door. His pipe was in his mouth. Mann brushed past him and went inside. The islander's wife stood at the table, a large sack tied about her waist, and her broad hands deep in powdered dough. Mann turned to Callum.

"Send your children to fetch the men of this island," he said. "I've some orders for them."

Callum had not moved from the door. He stood there with the rain blowing on the floor, and his hands across his stomach. Grun stood with his back to the fire eating, he had picked up a bannock from the hot tray on the hearth-stone. He looked curiously at Mann and the islander, and then thrust more of the warm cake into his mouth and ate it appreciatively. He swallowed the last of it and then took another and began to eat that. He did all this while Mann and Callum stared at one another. "Look," he said, "white flour."

"Shut up, you fool!" said Mann, and drew his pistol. "Send your children," he said again to Callum.

"You canna give us orders," said the old man.

"*Send your children!*"

The islander did not move. Mann felt his cheeks grow suddenly hot, and the hand that held the pistol trembled. Callum was looking at him calmly, his hands still in his pockets and his eyes sunk deeper in his face. The rain began to shine on the floor, and it beaded the side of the old man's face, clung to his hair, and stained the sleeve of his jacket. He swayed a little in the wind which, as if delighted to find an open door, gathered itself up and roared through the opening. The air of the room began to fill with flour. Grun stopped eating, another mouthful half-lifted in the air.

Suddenly the woman spoke to the children, and they darted past their father's legs into the open. He looked at his wife sadly and went across to a bench by the nets and sat down on it, with his hands drooping between his knees. The door was still open, and Mann looked through it, up along the paved footpath to the other cottages. He watched the children go from cottage to cottage, and the men leave soon after. They came into the room cautiously, glancing at Callum by the wall, and the two airmen standing in front of the fire with their pistols.

"Is that all, any more?" asked Mann, and Callum shook his head.

"Listen to me carefully," said Mann, raising his voice. "We will have the boat repaired. We want it done before the storm breaks."

Callum stood up. "No!" he said, but Mann ignored him.

"We realise that these boats of yours are valuable, and we'll allow three of you to repair the one on the shore."

The room was quite silent then. Mann felt uncomfortable. Before him the islanders, crowded in the small space, stooping some of them to avoid the low ceiling, looked at him coldly.

"How many will do it?" asked Mann.

One man spoke: "You mean you'll let us put to sea?"

Callum answered. He stood up again and pushed his way to the front and said quietly to Mann. "You're leaving us. You came and brought your guns and killed one of us, and now, just as suddenly you are going. But the boats were ours. You wouldn't move them and the sea destroyed them. I was glad, and now you want the last one repaired so that you can get away, and you think we're daft enough to do it for you."

Mann said finally: "Until the boat is repaired no one will draw water from the stream."

"Then no one shall draw water," said Callum. He turned to the islanders, "Don't let them go. They were lying when they said they had friends on the mainland. They're alone. We aren't the prisoners now. They are! For all their guns, they are our prisoners now, they canna get away."

Mann took him roughly by the shoulders, and pushed him aside. "Let them speak," he said. "What about it?" and he turned to the others.

"We need water," said one.

"There are children," said another.

"They are going to give themselves up to the military," said the old man with a satisfied thump of his stick.

Callum shook Mann's hand from his shoulder. "Don't do it. What's water? Is it cheaper than a boy's life?"

"But they're going to give themselves up," said the old man irritably. "The military will handle them."

"Look at yon man's face," said Callum, pointing at Mann "Does it look as if he's going to give himself up?" He pointed at Grun now, who stared at him suspiciously, "Or yon? He's afraid to give himself up, but he knows that he's going home!"

Mann grasped him by the jersey and held him there. "Have no doubt that we'll make you do it." He looked at his watch. "Work must commence on the boat within the next two hours," he said and closed the cover of his watch. He looked at the islanders and his voice softened slightly. "I do advise you to do this, although I came here with orders. You don't like us, and I can't expect you to, but this is war and we came here as soldiers and will act as soldiers always. But you would be wiser to do this, it's just my advice."

No one answered him and he was ashamed of his show of weakness. "See that you're there!" he said roughly, and motioned to Grun to follow him. The islanders made way for them without a word.

"Will they do it?" asked Grun outside, working his tongue about his teeth to pick out the cake crumbs.

"I don't know," said Mann. "They hate us."

"They frighten me."

Mann smiled. "Why? They're weak, you know."

"Yes, but they hate us. We do terrible things to them wherever we go, it's like an avalanche, because we have to go on doing them. It's our weapon and to stop people wresting it from us we must go on using it more and more ruthlessly. Everywhere, Mann, everywhere we go. You can't walk down a street we take without feeling that the people hate us and would kill us. It'll go and get worse when they realise that we're afraid of them too."

"You're part of the weapon," said Mann impatiently. "You don't shout 'Stop!' when you see it being used."

"I know," said Grun wearily, and he seemed to drop down below his collar with weariness. "We've got to go on doing these things, I suppose, because they'll have no mercy for us when we weaken. I think that some day they might be stronger than us and will try to wipe us out."

"Where?"

"Everywhere, and that frightens me, there's no way out of it. . . ."

"Perhaps not," said Mann. "But the woman told me that if we had come as friends they would have welcomed us," he smiled cynically. "If we'd brought them fruit, and silk blouses that the women could wear, and went fishing with them when the sea was smoother. And perhaps nesting for eggs." He pushed the pistol back in its holster. "My son would like this island, he's never really seen the sea. Where we live there are only long docks, and smoke from the ships, and great derricks. He plays by the canals. He'd like this island."

Grun looked at him queerly. "What were you talking to that woman about? Was it about all that?"

"No," said Mann. "It was nothing, perhaps I imagined it all. But they'll come to repair the boat, and we shall go home again."

The pilot met them at the door.

"Well?"

"It's hard to say. The old man is against it, but I think that some of them will agree. I gave them two hours to decide, with your permission."

"That's satisfactory." The pilot looked at his watch. "But if they won't come, we'll hold the old man as a hostage until someone does."

"It's because the boy was killed that they are like this," said Mann without warning.

"Then they'll discover that death can be deliberate as well as accidental." The pilot felt himself losing patience with the islanders. Hitherto he had been thankful for the passive way they had accepted the presence of himself and his men, but now he found it irritating, as if he sensed in it an opposite to his own character and resented it for that reason alone. It was not pleasant to leave the island and to admit partial defeat, to leave the islanders without full realisation of the power and importance of himself and his duty. Logically he had decided for ruthless insistence on obedience, and equally logically he was prepared to carry it out. He did not like Mann's expression.

"Grun," he said, "stand by this gun, and, Mann, I want to speak to you."

Mann followed the pilot into the other room, the room with the flowerless geranium in the window, the tiled floor, the hard chairs, and the fading wallpaper. The pilot went to the table and sat himself at it as he might a desk. He did not look at Mann, but took out his cigarette case. But without opening it he knew that it was empty and he slapped it sharply on the palm of his hand, and thrust it back into his tunic. He straightened the medal ribbon and put his hands together.

"Mann," he said, "what is your attitude toward these people?"

The navigator immediately felt that danger lay in the conversation that was to follow. He was standing to attention with his arms rigidly at his side. It was an uncomfortable position that imprisoned him physically and allowed his thoughts and his tongue no freedom either. His neck began to ache because he was keeping his head upright and yet looking down at the lieutenant. He knew that so long as he kept his eyes on the officer's face the pilot would not look at him, and perhaps thereby he might be at some advantage. The pilot was clicking the tips of his finger-nails together irritably. Mann, opening his mouth in an attempt to dissuade the suspicion and dangerous curiosity that lay behind the pilot's question, found that he could say nothing.

The pilot looked up sharply and said: "Answer my question!"

"I don't understand it, Herr Leutnant."

"You don't? I'll put it simply. Have you any sympathy for them?"

"No, Herr Leutnant."

It was not a ready answer, there had been a pause before Mann spoke, and the pilot felt that his suspicions were confirmed. Mann was evading honesty by direct denial. It pleased the lieutenant to prove that he had been correct in distrusting Mann, but he felt alarmed. For the first time he began to realise the reliance he had to place on these men, and his own sense of lonely responsibility. For a moment he nearly begged Mann not to desert him, but then his emotions became colder, more self-possessed. Hart was reliable, but foolish. Grun a megalomaniac. But Mann was the keystone that had to be assured.

"I don't believe you," he said. "I don't believe you, because last night you allowed a woman to leave her cottage and approach you on the jetty. You talked to her and let her go back and yet you made no report about the matter." He watched the navigator carefully as he spoke, and now that the position had been reversed, now that the initiative and confidence had passed to the pilot, it was Mann who felt lost and weaker. He stared above the pilot's head at the fireplace, and felt his face grow hotter. "I saw this," said the pilot, "and waited for you to make a report to me about it. You didn't do it, but," and the words came quickly and abruptly, "I want it now."

"The woman came to me to find out whether we would leave the island. She wanted you to let them repair the boat and hand us over to the enemy."

"What did you say?"

"I said it was impossible, and told her to go back."

"Did she go?"

"No, Herr Leutnant."

"What did you say then?"

"I said it was my orders to fire."

"And did she go then?"

"No, Herr Leutnant."

"Why didn't you fire?"

Mann felt the room growing larger, the walls were fading away about him, and he and the lieutenant were alone in a vast black space, he and a little man crouched before him in a suit with shining buttons.

"Why didn't you open fire, I said?"

"She was just a foolish woman, Herr Leutnant. She was just frightened, that's all."

"It wasn't your position to decide her motives, but to obey an order."

Mann wished he could relax the tension of his body. He felt that he could make the lieutenant understand so much better were he not encased in this armour of taut muscles. The officer's calm embarrassed him.

"I've never killed a woman, Herr Leutnant."

The pilot stood up quickly. He leaned forward on the table,

resting on the knuckles of his hands. The skin of his face was
drawn so tight that it almost erased the cleft in his chin.

"Killing, Korporal Mann," he said sarcastically, "is fashion-
able now. All over Europe there are people who place explosives
beneath the trains that carry your comrades to the front. They
shoot at your officers in cafés, they adulterate the food you eat,
they sabotage the machines you take into the air. And many of
them, Korporal Mann, are women. Women do not mind if you
crash to earth in a plane they have damaged. Women do not
mind if you are poisoned from foul food. Women do not mind if
you rot with the syphilis you catch from them. They do it because
they hate you. They do not share your chivalrous objections to
this new fashion of killing, and I don't intend to indulge in them
myself. We didn't come to this island to trade compliments or
flowers, Korporal Mann, but to help win a war. When I decide
that you should open fire you will do so, whether it's against a
woman or a man." He leaned back and breathed quickly. "Do
you understand?"

He sat down and, still breathing heavily, pulled at the collar
of his tunic, just as he had done when Mann told him about the
radio set. He was angry. He hated Mann, he hated him because
he relied on him still.

Mann did not answer. He could see the officer's figure before
him and felt that it was something unfamiliar, with which he
could not possibly have any relationship. It was a medium-sized
young man with fair hair and an old face, a medal ribbon and
the glitter of many buttons. He felt so old, as if he had seen so
much before he met this man and was to see so much after. He
felt as if he had been whirling about in a circle, and for a moment
this man in the tailored uniform had caught his sleeve to stop the
momentum. He felt tired, but the sense of whirling increased.

Once again the pilot placed his knuckles on the table, but this
time he did not rise.

"*Do you understand me?*"

"Yes, Herr Leutnant."

The tone of the reply was resigned, and relief flooded into the
lieutenant with refreshing suddenness. For a moment it had been
as if everything in which he believed had been challenged, and

now that had been dispelled. A note of amiability tinged his voice from then on. It was over now.

Mann felt giddy.

He was a tall man, and when he stood before a man who was seated the sense of height was enormous. Far below him, it seemed, was the lieutenant, a polished young man to whom everything was clear. But such a little man, a little, little man. But it was all clear to him, and the killing of a woman a small matter.

The pilot was aware of the navigator's height because he was looking up to it. A tall man with a triangular, scowling face, and thin hair that was never parted, a uniform that fitted loosely and resentfully. The pilot did not like looking into Mann's eyes. It had not the same effect that it had on Hart or Grun.

"Where do you come from, Mann?"

"From Hamburg, Herr Leutnant."

"We have done much for that," said the lieutenant, and he brushed on to other matters, looking at his watch. "Another hour. If no one comes, arrest the leader and the other boy, and tell the rest that unless the work is begun the old man will be shot."

The face relaxed. Things were becoming easier to understand. The cleft in his chin darkened to a deep gash. "If they are obstinate the boy will be shot. But I don't think that will be necessary. Now go and get some sleep, Mann," he concluded solicitously. "There's still time. You look tired. It's been hard on all of us, but we've done well. They'll be proud of us."

"Yes, Herr Leutnant. Thank you."

V

WHEN the hour was over two men came. Mann had not rested, but had stood by the door looking out at the rain, watching the cottages. Embedded in the earth, they resisted the weather firmly and only the dark stains of the rain showed on their white walls. Mann felt sure someone would come. He did not think that the islanders would be so stupid as to ignore the order. He just wondered which one it would be.

And then, far down towards the end of the line of cottages, a door opened, and a man stood in the doorway looking up at the sky and turning up his coat collar. He stepped out into the rain and thrust his hands in his pockets, turning back to look at the doorway. A second man came out, struggling into his coat, the collar of which he too turned up, and then with their hands in the pockets and their shoulders hunched, they moved across the rough earth to Mann. They did not look back at the cottages, but walked sullenly, not even turning when another door opened and a woman's voice screamed at them. There was queer tumult in their faces. They marched up to Mann and said resentfully.

"We've come. What do you want done?"

Mann looked over his shoulder. The officer was standing behind him. He was smiling.

"All right, Mann," he said, "Take them down and see what they can make of it."

The navigator pulled down his cap and told the men to follow him. The storm was getting stronger and the three men moved about the boat, pushing themselves against the wind and peering at the broken wood and the torn sail. The island was thick with sea-fowl that flew low, or sat on the rocks, their white and grey feathers livid and their wild skirling high above that of the wind. Down by the black rocks was the bloody well where the islanders gutted their fish, and this was thick with birds, although there was no offal there. The gulls waited patiently, and once the islanders by the boat stopped and looked at them. Mann thought he sensed what they were feeling. He had never seen so many birds, and he thought of his son who had never collected eggs, but who would do so on this island. And he thought of the boy's legs, thin and white, and how brown and round were those of the island children. He saw the bird's wings as they glided, the feathers outstretched like the fingers of a man's hands.

The islanders muttered to themselves, they passed their hands over the gash in the vessel's side and looked over the gunwale to the stump of the mast. They climbed inside and one of them picked up a net and then let it slide through his fingers. The rain ran down the crown of his bonnet to his nose, from where it dripped to his jacket. He took off the cap and wiped his forehead and face with the inside of it, and then, with it still in his hand, looked across to where Mann stood on the beach. He waited for the navigator to speak.

"Can you do it?" asked Mann.

"Aye," said the islander slowly.

"Start now?"

"Aye, we'll start, but we must get our tools from the house."

"Will it take long?"

"A day, maybe two. We canna work long in this weather."

"Right," said Mann, and he turned to walk back, and then stopped and looked over his shoulder at them. They had not moved. The islander had not replaced his bonnet, and his face was shining with rain. "The gun at the door can fire down here," Mann said without emotion.

"Aye," said the man in the boat, and pulled his bonnet over his eyes. "We know that."

Mann walked back. He had not gone far, bending his head down against the wind until his eyes could see only the wet stones and rivulets of sea-water on the shore, when he heard someone running after him. He turned quickly, fearful of a sudden blow in the back, and up at the cottage he heard a voice shout a warning.

It was the second islander. The man who had not spoken. He stopped when Mann turned, and he watched the navigator apprehensively, for the airman's hand rested on his pistol. He had a thin, dyspeptic face, and his eyes were hard like blue beach stones, shining with water. But his mouth was kindly and the brown skin about it creased by wrinkles.

"What do you want?" said Mann hoarsely, and then cleared his throat and spat away from the wind. He felt embarrassed.

The islander raised his hand and let it drop to his side.

"Alan . . ." he began. "My brother wanted to ask you. . . . The boat. . . ."

"What about it?"

"You're letting us repair it, but will you be letting us take her to sea, now?"

"I can't tell you," Mann's voice was still harsh and he cleared his throat again nervously.

WHERE THE SEA BREAKS

"What are you going to do with her?" The islander eyed him cunningly, and ran his tongue gently along his lower lip.

"I can't tell you!" said Mann angrily.

"If you're taking her away you'll be paying us for a new one, man, won't you? She's the only one left on the island."

Mann flushed. "We're not bargaining with you!" he shouted. "The boat must be repaired, or you'll both be held responsible. Do you understand?"

"Aye," said the man, and went back to his brother.

Mann climbed up to the cottages, wondering why he felt so angry with the two islanders, knowing that they were staring at him, resenting his refusal to bargain with them. He had expected someone to come, and now that they had he felt vaguely disturbed and even ashamed because of it. It was with surprise that he realised that he would rather no one had come.

When he got to the cottage, the pilot called him.

"Well?"

"They'll do it. They've gone for the tools. It'll take them a day or two, though."

"Good." The pilot picked his teeth delicately with his finger-nail. "What did that fellow want who ran after you. He was lucky I didn't shoot him."

Mann felt himself flushing. "They wanted to bargain over the price of the boat," he said.

The pilot laughed and ran his fingers across the ribbon on his chest. "The price?" he said, and looked at Mann for a moment and then went inside his room and shut the door.

There was the noise of footsteps outside. It was the islanders going back to their cottage. They glanced at the doorway, and it seemed as if one of them wanted to stop, but his arm was grasped by the other and they went on to their own cottage. This time no one screamed at them, there was no sign or sound from the other cottages.

VI

GRUN was drunk. Stern's brandy was all gone and all the world and its darkness had sped away with it. Grun was happy, and he sat and let the wind blow through the cottage door and sting his face with rain. He laughed and giggled, and stood up now and then to strut out into the rain and preen himself against the storm. It was black outside, and within the blackness the noise of the storm and the rolling thunder of the sea against the island.

Oh yes, he was drunk, and he knew it. He felt the reeling stupor of it, the crazy exhilaration and insane conquest of it. He swelled up inside until his body wanted to burst out of its uniform. His mouth fell open and took in the cold wind to burn his lungs.

Perhaps to sit there at the gun and drowse, and perhaps to jump up and swagger out and shout at the storm. Perhaps to do neither of these, but think cunningly how stupid were these people who could think of nothing but submission and defeat.

And the boat, there had been hammering there on the beach that day. Two men in thick blue jerseys, with crude tools, carefully and lovingly building over the gash in the boat's side, and Grun, standing on the jetty beside Hart, had watched them gleefully. Every nail meant a yard nearer home, every splinter planed down was an ugliness smoothed out of the life he had been living. He grinned and the grin widened and split his face. He nodded stupidly and thought of the boat. It was escape. To the lieutenant it was expediency, but to him it was escape, and he was glad.

He did not want to pray and he wished he could have the courage to go over to the cottage where Hart had gone, and then he began to weep because it was sinful to think like that, and he began to pray very hard, asking, with every hoarse sentence, for absolution. He grew more and more sorry for himself, and wept. But the fierce, fuming brandy swamped the maudlin sentiments, and Grun hugged his knees. The brandy burnt inside his head like a fire. It had orange flames, black-lipped flames like burning oil, and they dipped and eddied like a candle in the draught. And the noise inside Grun's head was enormous. He held it between his hands and seemed to shut out the orange glow. He felt sick.

His body, slack and useless, was seized roughly. It was Mann shaking him.

"You drunken idiot! Wake up, what's happening to the boat? Where's Hart?"

Grun rolled away. "So many questions at once. Let me alone and go to bed. Go to hell!"

"The boat's burning. Do you hear? *The boat is burning!*"

Grun giggled. He sputtered as if he were enjoying a foolish joke. He could not see Mann in the dark and his head ached, but it was a funny joke.

Mann flung him over the gun and ran out into the open. The wind caught him immediately and blew him joyously toward the burning vessel. Grun lay over the gun and laughed, and wept and was sick in turn. The muzzle of the gun pointed upward with the weight of his body, and the bolt grazed his cheek until it bled.

Mann came back. In the light of the flames his face was alarming. The rain had combed his hair over his forehead and parted it there in three spikes. He grasped Grun and pulled him upright. The drunken man's head, pulled back by the roughness of the action, flopped over his neck and the mouth hung open. Grun belched. He tried to say something, but his giggling drowned it.

"*Where's Hart?*" shouted Mann urgently. "There's no one at the gun. Where's Hart?"

Grun made no reply. His tongue lolled happily at Mann, and the navigator flung him once more at the gun.

Mann stood up. It was impossible now to put out the flames. Despite the storm, they ate into the vessel hungrily. Pitch had been smeared over the woodwork, and now it bubbled and burnt. The wind occasionally blew the embers of the sail-cloth at him, carrying the rich pungency of a fire. Mann pushed at his wet hair. He was seriously alarmed.

He did not notice the officer until his arm was grasped. In the light, the unsteady leaping light, Mann saw that the pilot had not dressed. He stood there in his underclothes and boots, the blonde hair on his chest glinting, and the cleft dark in his chin. He held a revolver in his hand.

"What is it?"

"The boat's burning."

The officer swore, looked at the drunken Grun and kicked him violently.

"It's no good," said Mann. "He's unconscious."

The pilot swore again and rushed out from the door. Mann followed him. The officer's boots were unlaced, and as he ran he swore at them too. The two airmen dropped from the jetty and stumbled across to the boat. It glowed from the inside. Mann realised that a great deal of pitch must have been placed there. The heart of it glowed, and was flecked with white, and its flames, bent like trees before a wind, rose about the deck, the broken mast, and the prow. The sail had gone, and now scraps of it, still burning, swept away before the wind. The fire leaned away from the storm, it pointed itself inward to the island and beat and sang with fierce heat.

And before it the officer in his underclothes, with his pistol in his hand, stood and swore. His legs were thin and the bottom of his underclothes were loose and fluttered silently. He too, like the fire, bent away from the gust of the storm that rode in with the waves. The right arm was bent to shelter the face, and that too was thin. He looks ridiculous, thought Mann.

The effect of the burning vessel was overpowering. It stunned the pilot. He stood and looked at it incredulously. His face, his chest, and his belly were scorched, his back shivered in the rain. He wanted to fire his pistol into the fire, but the hand that held it would not move. And he knew that it was not only the boat that was being destroyed there.

The patch of red light from the vessel spread up the hillside and picked out the white cottages. It spread out to sea too, and Mann could see the waves coming in unheedingly, high, rolling, and white. They tipped over and crashed on the pebbles and fought their long battle with the island.

In every cottage window there was a lamp, and Mann could see people at the doors. Every door was open and light from them flooded on to the heather. The rain shone in the light like metal. The island was alight. Light from the burning boat, from the windows and open doors, and the pilot still stood in his underclothes staring at the fire.

Suddenly the fascination broke and he turned, rushed past Mann and began to stumble back to the cottage. He was breathing heavily, but he moved quickly and Mann found it hard to keep up with him. He reached the cottage and dragged Grun's body from the gun, squatting behind it with his vest now wide open and the swastika ring on his finger gleaming black and white.

He aimed the gun at the cottages and began to fire. The quick, confident sound of the shots awakened a memory in Mann, it seemed to stabilise things. The shots did no damage, but the lights disappeared quickly from the cottage windows, the doors were closed, but the pilot continued firing, and Mann stood by and fed the belt into the gun automatically.

Just before the gun stopped, Mann heard the sound of a breaking window and a woman shouting. At last the pilot stood up. There was rain in his face and his eyes were blood-shot. He looked at Grun and spat in the man's face. He looked at Mann, but did not seem to recognise him. He got up and began to fasten the buttons of his underclothes. The fingers twitched at the cloth nervously, but could not fasten it, and the wool gaped disgustingly down the length of his body. Mann found himself looking at him critically. For the first time he saw the officer as a laughable spectacle.

And Grun lying with his body half out of the door, the back of his head in a muddy puddle, snored happily.

The pilot ended his wild staring abruptly by turning and entering his room. Mann sat down at the gun and swiftly fed another belt into it. Then he pulled Grun into the shelter of the room and slumped him in a corner. The wireless operator quarrelled and laughed with himself in his stupor. The vessel still burned, but its flames were dying, and on it, in its decline, the storm descended. The ceaseless roar of the wind, which had not subsided since they came there five days ago, echoed in Mann's brain, and he worked quickly at the gun to shut out the noise of it, and the thoughts that the burning boat had disturbed. At length the gun was ready, and Mann sat at it patiently, watching the other houses.

The pilot came out again. He was fastening the bottons of his tunic, and this time his fingers were steady, but he had forgotten to put on his cap, and he had not combed his hair. He was not calm.

" Hart. . . . Where is Hart?"

Mann did not look up from the gun. "I couldn't find him. He wasn't on the jetty, and the gun had been tipped over the edge into the sea. He must have seen the flames. . . ."

Then he did look up, and the one stared back at the other, not wishing to say what was in their minds. The pilot sat down on his heels beside Mann. He seemed lonely.

"What was it, Mann? Who started the fire, those two men?"

"I don't know, Herr Leutnant, but it seemed as if there were something inflammable in the hull. It was burning strongly."

"Yes . . ." said the lieutenant, and bit at his fingernail. "Light the lamp and bring it in here. Put it behind the door so that we won't show up against it." He looked out into the storm. "There's only us now, Mann. Grun is useless, his nerve's gone. There's only us now, Mann."

Mann felt sick and heavy with weariness. He wanted to shake the lieutenant as he had shaken Grun. They should go out to look for Hart, but the lieutenant stayed by the gun, and his fingers played and fidgeted over the breech.

"We must decide what to do now, Mann. The boat's gone and they think we're caught. But we still have the gun and we will be the strongest yet."

He looked at Mann, peering through the dim light, trying to catch some hint of what Mann was thinking, and then he looked quickly away.

They sat there until dawn, until the darkness faded into a sickly yellow light, and the sky over the sea was heavy. The island still fought the storm. Mann ached with fatigue, his clothes were wet and stiff where they had creased, and the fumes from the drunken operator were stifling. Grun awoke just after dawn. His body did not move, but slowly his eyelids were lifted, and his eyes stared out of the white skin and over the open mouth at Mann and the pilot. His back rested against the wall and his feet splayed out in their heavy boots. His tunic was open and a little crucifix gleamed on his shirt. He breathed heavily and the tip of his tongue rested lightly in the corner of his mouth. When the pilot turned and saw him he got up and went over, grasping the operator by the shoulder. Grun tried to get up, but the pilot forced him down to the floor and looked hard into his face. The nerves at the side of the pilot's mouth twitched. The arm that was extended was taut and the knuckles white. Finally, he pushed Grun from him in distaste and went over to the door, where he stood, nervously, with his hands behind his back, pushing the palm of one against the other.

Mann wished he could smoke, but there were no more cigarettes on the island. Nor could he hope for something to eat. Two days ago the woman who had cooked for them had gone and refused to return, and Grun had done it, but now he lay against the wall, too frightened to get up, belching occasionally and playing with the cross at his throat.

The pilot turned, he was more self-possessed, his back was straighter and he had pushed his fingers through his hair.

"Mann," he said, "bring that drunken sot to his senses and go and find Hart. When you've done that, bring me the leader of these people." His lips were thin, and the cleft in his chin far more shallow than usual. "We have ceased to be gentlemen."

Mann went over and knelt on one knee beside Grun. He slapped him hard on either side of the face, and the wireless operator began to cry. He sagged forward against Mann and wept. Mann let him cry for a while and then shook him and pulled him to his feet. Grun looked at the navigator and big tears rolled down his dirty cheeks, his lower lip hung loosely. Mann shook him brutally until he stopped crying.

"Hit him again," said the lieutenant.

Mann looked over his shoulder at the officer, holding Grun by the front of his tunic.

"Hit him again!"

Mann released his hold on the wireless operator and wiped both palms of his hands simultaneously on his trousers. He eased his neck with a convulsive little jerk and pushed back his hair.

"All right now?" he said, and Grun nodded and choked.

The lieutenant pushed past Mann and seized Grun by both shoulders. He shook the man until Grun's mouth dropped open and the crucifix fell from his neck beneath the pilot's boots. He went on shaking and shaking, getting more and more furious, his face red and his lips wet with saliva. Grun's face began to assume a look of imbecility, and he was crying again.

The lieutenant was swearing at him, and saying over and over, "It's your fault, your fault!"

Sobbing, Grun caught his breath hysterically like a woman. Mann felt uncomfortable, and he picked up Grun's cap and held it out to the wireless operator. The action seemed to sober the lieutenant, for he let go of Grun and walked quickly to the other room. Mann heard the chair creak as he flung himself into it.

"Grun," he said softly, "pull yourself together; this won't do." But the other man went on shaking, as if the pilot's fury had set off a motion that had not yet exhausted its impetus. He held out his hands before Mann, as if he wanted the navigator to grasp them.

"Grun," said Mann, "what's the matter? This won't do."

"I'm afraid." The words were almost incoherent.

"It won't do," said Mann again. "We can't afford to lose our nerves."

"Where's Hart? Who burnt the boat? Why does he blame me?"

"Because you were drunk, you fool," said Mann angrily. "You went to sleep and someone got out of the cottages and burnt the boat. Can't you understand what has happened?"

Grun nodded miserably. He looked out through the door at the rain and the heather, aborted in its growth away from the wind. He looked over to the cottages, to the benches outside their doors, shining black, to the oars held on the walls in crude saltire, the small curtained windows and low roofs, the chimneys and the threads of smoke held straight from them by the wind. He looked behind them, up the hill to the long walls, the yellow chrysanthemums and rough ploughed earth. The pigs were squealing in the sty and a cock crowed to the sun that had risen behind the storm.

"What will they do?" he asked.

"It's a game," said Mann coldly. "They have made their move, and now its ours. We go on making moves until the game is over, and the one who is the more cunning, the faster and the strongest wins."

Grun looked at him, his eyes were hostile. "You don't see it like I do," he said.

Something seemed to burst inside Mann and he fought with it, something that wanted to protest, to bully, to brush aside accusation. It was useless, and he suddenly felt deflated. He shrugged his shoulders.

"Get yourself properly dressed," he said. "We've got to find Hart, and then arrest the leader."

"The next move," said Grun bitterly. "*Hostages!* It's not very original, it is?"

"Well, what would you do?"

"The same. It's a game, isn't it? You said so." He grinned. "But they've got so many, many pieces to spare. Here on this island, and everywhere, and we go on, logically knocking them off the board. But each time there are many of them to spare." He began to laugh now, he held his hands on his cheeks and opened his mouth as he laughed. His teeth were bad.

"Shut up," said Mann quietly.

"It's easy to say 'shut up,' isn't it?" sneered Grun. "Especially when you shut out of your own mind what's going on. Shut up!" he mimicked. "Shut up! *Shut up!*"

"The lieutenant told me to hit you just now," said Mann. "I didn't do it. I don't know why. But I shall hit you if you don't shut up."

Grun snorted bitterly and began to button up his tunic. He pushed his hair beneath his cap and faced Mann, who looked at him critically.

"Take your pistol," he said. "And for God's sake look like a man."

He knocked on the door of the pilot's room. It was a rough door, and there were children's initials carved on it near the floor, and a date, and within his gaze as he looked at them Mann could see his heavy military boots. He looked up nervously as the pilot opened the door.

"We're leaving now, Herr Leutnant."

"Good, I'll cover you with the gun. Have you a whistle?"

"No."

"Take this one. Blow it if you have to and I'll do what I can. Find Hart first and then report to me. If the leader or anyone else"—he lifted the corner of his mouth—"man or woman, attempts to leave the cottage to follow you, I shall shoot."

Mann nodded, he did not salute, and he went out, lowering his head beneath the lintel, and brushing his legs against the machine gun on the floor.

VII

THE lieutenant sat by the gun, lightly picking his teeth with his fingernail. "Pork-butcher's suckling" Stern had called him, because of his pink skin and fair hair, and more than ever before he resented the title. He put the blame on Stern for all this, switching it from Grun to the second pilot because of the flask of brandy which, he realised, the operator must have taken from the dead man's pocket.

But he forgot quickly. He was certain that Mann would find Hart's body, and when they came back with it the long period of waiting would be ended. He was determined to go on shooting until they found the murderer, and then he would be shot too. Mann would be executioner.

The pilot stretched out his legs and left his teeth alone. Mann would be executioner.

The islanders seemed remote, black figures with no character, and he felt jealous of Mann because he could understand their language, jealousy that was mixed with deep suspicion. But he did not know the islanders, did not understand the look in their eyes, did not like the feelings that radiated from them. He told himself it was not fright he felt, but anger and hatred, and he could not bring himself to think of them without embarrassment.

The thought of leaving the island persecuted him, he did not know how it was to be done now that the boat had been destroyed, and in an effort to liquidate the thought he got up and switched on the radio, hoping for helpful news. But they were playing regimental marches and there was singing. The heavy, thudding rhythm of the march kept in step with the beat of his heart.

He went back to the gun and sat down beside it. Soon the marches were over and were followed by soft waltzes with deep, caressing melodies. The pilot beat time to them with his fingers on the cocking handle of the gun. He felt sentimentally moved by the music.

VIII

SOMETIMES the islanders would take their catch to the mainland, where they sold it along the quays. Then they saw it no more, and went back to the island with their decks filmed by the silver scales and the hulls high above the water. But sometimes they brought it to the island, and the women came out of the cottages with high boots on, jerseys rolled up above their fat elbows, short knives in their hands. And the children went with them, and all of them gutted and cleaned the fish by the black rocks, standing ankle deep in the water and taking the fish from the shallow pools where they had been poured. Then they were barrelled in salt and the lids hammered down upon them. And a boy painted the islanders' names in white upon the lids, painted them in bold, childish letters, with dots above the capital "I's" and an occasional "s" lettered backwards.

The heads and red guts the women flung behind them, to a pile that grew in volume and stench as they worked. The women sang as they worked, high, lilting songs, while the men swilled off the decks and mended nets. And as the women sang the wind took the smell of blood out to sea, and the gulls came in, came in revolving spheres that circled beautifully in powerful glides. Then they would drop to the pile of guts, sharp beaks thrusting critically at the food, the slimes oozing through their strong talons.

The shallow pools were floored with silver sand, the rocks draped with the tendrils of seaweed and dotted with bird droppings. When the tide came in it cleaned the place and took out to sea a scab of guts, with its hovering, floating escort of fowl.

The islanders called this place the "Gutter", and it was here that the airmen found Hart.

Mann and Grun came upon him by accident. They did not expect to find him there, if they expected to find him at all. Mann found the search ominous. He knew that he could expect no help from the islanders, and the atmosphere was tense. Earlier they had dragged the machine gun from the wash of the sea and re-established it on the jetty, where it now stood, dangerously alone. He wondered why the islanders had not destroyed it, or why they had not turned it upon the airmen. There was much he did not understand, and behind him, as they moved about the winded slope of the island, Grun shuffled and talked to himself.

They climbed the fields behind the cottages, searching the walls and the outhouses, where the pigs grunted contentedly at them and the chickens fled in a flurry of wings. Mann wanted to delay the approach to the islanders until the last moment. At times he thought that perhaps the position of hostages had been reversed, and that Hart was in one of the cottages somewhere. But the idea seemed unreal. All seemed unreal.

They could feel the eyes of the islanders upon them, looking at them from behind the curtains, behind the soft green leaves of the geraniums and the rain dribbling down the panes. The wet grass stained their boots and breeches, and the salt of the spray that whirled in clouds over the island, indistinguishable from the rain, bit into their skins and burnt their necks.

They had one interesting discovery. In a small, walled garden at the rear of one of the cottages, Mann thought it was Callum's, they found a tiny dinghy. It lay overturned beneath a tangle of old nets and tarpaulin. Mann tore these from it excitedly. When he saw it, it was as if a great weight had fallen from his spirit and his blood throbbed suddenly with the thought of his home and his wife. It was a small boat and undamaged, a boat that might trail dog-like from the stern of a larger vessel. A number was painted in white on the bows and it smelt of pitch and fish. Mann looked at it critically. He did not believe that the islanders had meant to hide it. The grass that it revealed was white and sickly, it had been there some time. He wondered whether it would live on its own out there on the sea, and the weight fell on him again as he realised that it probably would not.

And once, as they looked at the boat, he heard the door of the cottage open, but before he could look up it was closed and he heard the bolt shoot home. A curtain flickered, a voice spoke, and he felt alone on the island with no one to understand his thoughts. Even Grun was an enemy.

Then they found Hart.

They had passed all the cottages and climbed, almost instinctively, to the black rocks of the Gutter. They came upon the air gunner suddenly, looked down on him from the ridge of stone.

Hart lay on his belly with his arms crooked and his legs splayed out, as if he had swum in from the sea and collapsed there from exhaustion. But now and then the waves swept in over him and until they retired he was lost beneath their tumult, and then there he was again, his long hair washed this way and that by the eddying water, his clothes shining and one boot missing. The sea sucked the sand from beneath his body and made a shallow, open grave for it. There was green sea-moss on his tunic, and his head, loose at the neck, flopped from one side to the other with the hesitant rush of water.

They climbed down to him, halted once by the waves that burbled and swirled up to them resentfully, and eventually they dragged him up to where the tussocks began, and only the spray could reach them. They turned him over. His mouth was open, his eyes hidden behind clotted sand, and blood was where the rest of his face had been. He was quite dead and unpleasant to look at. Grun began to pray excitedly:

"*Pater noster, qui es in coelis, sanctificetur nomen tuum. . . .*"

"Shut up!" said Mann quickly, and he began to empty Hart's pockets. There was little there, identification, a letter or two, blurred photographs that still held some detail of their obscenity, and some money. And he was heavy with water that flowed from his mouth as they turned his body or put weight upon it. But he had not been drowned. He had been struck on the head.

Mann stood up and wiped his hands thoughtfully on his

trousers in an old gesture. He looked worried, and Grun noticed how thin he suddenly seemed, as if his body had been drawn taut.

"I know why," said Grun.

"Of course, they had to," said Mann, as if washing the excuse aside.

"But you *don't* know," went on Grun hurriedly. "It was the woman."

"What woman?"

"The one in the cottage opposite us, the good-looking one. The one who was singing, Hart said. He wanted her, he kept on talking about her as he always talked about women, and then one evening he went across there. He came back and played cards with me and won, he always did after things like that. That's my money you took from his pocket. It's no good to him now. Give it back to me."

Mann took him by the collar angrily. "Never mind the bloody money. What about the woman?"

Grun shook him off. "I told him what would happen, but he went on playing and winning, and boasting, and telling me all about it. He said she never fought, and he didn't really enjoy it because of that, I think. But he wouldn't believe anything would happen." Grun's voice rose a little. "He said they were afraid to do anything. He said, what were the women there for?"

He stopped and looked at Mann with his lip quivering. "How are we going to get back now?"

"The fool!" said Mann, and he sat down beside Hart's body, with his long arms hanging between his legs, but all he could say was: "I'd like a cigarette."

Grun looked at him in amazement. "Is that all it means to you?"

Mann looked up at him. "What do you expect me to say? I never liked him, you know that, so I can't feel sorry for him. After what he did you can understand why these people do things like this." He took a deep breath. "He asked for it. But it's not only that, he disobeyed orders. I don't like to think what's going to happen now."

Grun stared at him with open mouth. "Yes," he said in a

hoarse whisper, and then he began to shout: "It's started now, and we can't stop it. I told you it'd start. I told you!"

"Oh, shut up," said Mann, "or you'll be praying again."

Grun went red. "I have to. It helps me."

Mann looked at him shrewdly. "I'd like to believe you. I know it does some people, but I know it doesn't comfort you. You try to drown everything with your prayers. You think you're excusing everything, but you're still as frightened afterwards. You're better off when you drink."

Grun felt his bubble pricked.

"I know," he said, and he looked down at Hart. Mann thought he was going to cry again, and he felt sorry for him.

"I'm sorry, Grun. It's not easy to be pleasant with this at your feet. I've an idea. That small boat, when the storm drops, take it and try to get to the mainland and give yourself up."

Grun stared at him in amazement. "Why?"

"You'll be court-martialled when we get back. The lieutenant won't forget your drunkenness after this. You'll be safer if you go. You'll be all right, they'll look after you."

"You're mad," said Grun heatedly. "You're mad if you think we'll ever get away from here. It'll be the same for us as it was for Hart," and then he pleaded. "*Will* we ever get away?"

"Of course."

"Do you really believe it?"

"Of course," said Mann again, and looked down at his boots.

"I'm glad," said Grun simply.

The navigator looked at him curiously. "You won't take the boat?"

"No."

"You fool," said Mann firmly. "You're getting a chance and you won't take it."

"I daren't. I don't trust them. They hate us too much; this is our life, all this." He looked at Mann defiantly. "You're trying to frighten me. They won't do anything to me when we get back. When you come to look at it right, we've been heroes in a way. They don't punish heroes!"

Mann shrugged his shoulders. "You *are* a fool. You ought to know by now what to expect."

Disturbed by the airmen's arrival, the gulls had flown up into the air, protesting shrilly, the sound of their calls like the movement of an unoiled hinge, but now they took shelter again in the crannies of the rocks, and they watched the little group with their black eyes. Mann, in a moment of abstraction, tried to count them, but they were too many. They were big birds, as big as the few chicken behind the cottages, and their feathers were white, the colour of their legs a deep scarlet or pure orange. He wondered what they were like to eat, but remembered that sailors had told him they were greasy. And he wondered why he was thinking about things like that, so he stood up wearily.

"Help me to carry him back," he said. "The lieutenant will want to see him."

"Can't we bury him here? I don't want to carry him."

"Take hold of his feet," said Mann. "I said the lieutenant will want to see him."

It was not easy to carry him. The body was heavy and the wind wanted to resist their attempts to take it away. Once they had climbed out of the Gutter, the cottages were only a few hundred yards away, huddled down beneath the storm, and beyond them the blackened skeleton of the burnt vessel. Mann noticed how small the island seemed, encompassed by the rolling turbulence of the sea and wreathed in rain and spray. He could see the lieutenant sitting at the gun in the doorway, and although he could not see them he knew that the islanders were watching them bringing the body back. He felt foolish and weak, defeated.

And back at the cottage the lieutenant, if he thought about it, did not know whether to be alarmed or angry. He had expected the men to find Hart's body, and he had decided what to do next. He watched the clumsy, staggering approach of Mann and Grun, and the heavy sway of Hart's body between them. Yet had he really expected this much from the islanders? There were so few of them, no chance for opposition, for resistance underground, but that made retribution the easier. He was sorry in a way that it had been Hart they killed, but he accepted the loss philosophically. The old man must be arrested. They would shoot him because Hart had been killed, but if necessary, in the interests of justice, he must be held as a hostage for the production of the murderers, the men who had burnt the boat.

And, when he thought of the boat, back came the realisation that its wet embers symbolised the destruction of their chance of leaving the island. He had tried hard to think of an alternative, and had at last rejected the problem. They would stay. They would stay with their guns, and wait, because it was all that was left, and eventually there would be news from the radio. He quite believed that now. He kept it on all day, just in case, and he hoped the batteries would last. Behind him now, as he watched them bringing over Hart's body, it gently broadcast its soft waltzes, submerged occasionally in the cacophony of atmospherics. It made him feel safer, as if one hand was kept linked with his homeland while the other grasped the island. But although the announcer occasionally broke into the music, and although the announcements were sometimes celebrated with a tremendous chord of Wagnerian magnificence, there was never anything to which he could pin expectation.

And here, as the radio played, Mann and Grun brought the body of Hart.

He got up and let them pass, and they brought it into the room and laid it on the floor. The sea-water dripped from the hems of the uniform, and Hart's head, loose on the spine, looked silly and independent. Mann gave the pilot the letters and money, and watched him put them into his pocket.

"It's terrible," said the pilot. "He must have surprised them at the boat and they had to kill him."

Mann looked at Grun. Grun's face was alarmed, but Mann disregarded it. "It wasn't that," he said bluntly. "Hart had been across to the woman. They killed him for it."

The pilot felt that the awkwardness and unreality of the situation demanded point. He took out his handkerchief, shook it gently, and laid it across Hart's face.

"He died for his country," he said. "I don't think he would have asked for anything more than that." He did not seem to have heard what Mann had said, and the navigator watched the water and blood soaking through the handkerchief until the linen moulded itself about the rear-gunner's face. The pilot was white, but his hands were quite steady.

"And now," he said, "go and get the leader. Tell them that unless we have the murderers by dawn to-morrow, he will be shot."

"How about the boy, Herr Leutnant?"

"Did I include the boy? No, bring the leader only. But wait a minute . . . bring the boy too. No one worries much whether an old man lives or dies, but they will be too sentimental about the boy."

Mann stood to attention automatically as he received this order. He knew how taut muscles could stifle thought, and at this moment he did not want to think. He decided to tell the pilot about the boat.

"There is another boat on the island," he said. "A small thing that might carry three men at a pinch. It's behind the cottage over there, and undamaged."

The pilot looked angry, but he felt relieved. "Good," he said. "They won't be able to destroy that. Make the old man and the boy bring it here by the jetty, where we can watch it."

They went, and the pilot went in and turned up the radio. He felt elated by relief, and he moved his hand gently to the rhythm of the dance music.

THEY GO

I

IT was very dark in the little room above the cottage. It was hardly more than an attic, squeezed between the beams of the roof and the floor that was the ceiling of the pilot's room below, and through the dusty air and dirty windows the daylight was further grimed by the stormy sky. It had been the only place to put the prisoners, and Mann sat there at the door with a pistol on a box in front of him.

He had not spoken to them since he and Grun brought them there, and although he watched them all the time, they did not speak to him. He sat quite still, with his hands hanging between his knees, the long fingers bent and the knuckles standing out above the thin flesh.

It was an untidy room, littered by jumble gathered through several generations and long ago discarded, old furniture, picture frames that had rotted in the salt air, books and magazines tied in bundles and a great iron bedstead with its brass all tarnished, that leaned against the far wall like the gate of a house. And above all this, as Mann had already noticed about these cottages, was the smell of tar. He found it appealing.

But it was very dark in the room, and on the roof the rain and wind tore at the turf-thatch. Mann seemed to notice the noise of the storm here in this room far more than he had done outside, for it echoed like a drum roll, and he sensed the power and magnificence of the wind as it sang about the eaves and whistled down the crude drains, as if it were aiming rough, affectionate blows at the house. As if it only wanted to show its strength, a strength that could easily destroy the building did it desire. But Mann, looking at the stone walls, and feeling in his blood the chill air they encased, seeing the great depth of the window sill, knew that the wind was bluffing. The cottage had been built to survive such fury. It was really the cottage that had true power and strength, the wind was a bully.

He had been sitting there for a long time and he felt lonely.

Sometimes the old man and the boy spoke to each other, sometimes they tried to sleep. Mann wondered why the pilot had
thought that they might attempt to kill themselves, and he pon-
dered ironically on the orders that instructed him to shoot them
did they attempt such a thing. For they did not seem afraid of his
revolver, and the old man treated him respectfully. Only the boy
stared with hurt, angry eyes.

He listened to them sometimes when they spoke, and at others
he shut out of his mind their queer, lilting voices, and thought
instead of his home, or the wind above the cliffs, the eggs that
were in the nests there, and the collection they would make for
his son. And he thought too, when he could not suppress the
thought, of the woman with the rain staining her blouse, and how
Hart must have burst in on her, because he knew Hart and what
he must have done.

And as a background to these thoughts, was a depression he
could never relieve, the melancholy experience of four years of
life like this. It had been going on and on and he had ceased to
believe that one day it might stop.

The boy was about fourteen. He was long and gangling, and
his face filmed with light hairs. His eyes were close above a high
nose and his hair fell over his forehead. High boots came up his
calves, the elbows of his jersey were darned with grey wool, and
his pockets gaped with the twine and nails and stones that had
been stored there. He lay on his back with his hands behind his
head, and his legs splayed out, so that, to Mann, his body was
foreshortened behind the soles of the rubber boots. But Mann
knew that he was not at ease. He would have liked the boy to talk
to him, but he knew that he looked too stern, too unfriendly for
anyone to want to do that, and he felt restless because he wanted
to smoke and there were no more cigarettes.

When the boy spoke he did not look at the man beside him, he
looked straight at Mann, as if challenging the airman to listen.
And the old man, who sat on a chair by the boy, did not seem to
know that Mann was there.

"Bevan's wife has ordered the sow from the mainland," said
the boy, "but she won't know how to look after it. She'll let it get
out of the sty and it'll break its legs on the beach."

The old man smiled. "Bevan will be home next year, he told his wife to have the bacon."

"Mam's the only one on the island who can keep pigs. The rest of them think they're like fish and can look after themselves, but I clean out the sty for them and they don't want to get out. But the other night some daft fool must have climbed through the sty, Callum, because the boards were broken on one side and there were some footprints there."

The old man didn't smile. "It was one of the airmen," he said.

"The one they found in the Gutter."

"Probably."

"What was he doing in the sty?" The boy leaned over on one elbow and grinned a little at Mann. "Was he looking for his friends."

Callum looked sharply at Mann, and held out his hand in warning to the boy, but Mann did not move.

"I'm not afraid of *yon*," said the boy resentfully and he looked straight at the navigator. "I hope he heard me!"

Mann had heard him, and he wondered why he had no feelings at all. Just an emptiness. He should have been angry, he told himself, he should have hit the boy.

The boy was frowning, so that his eyes contracted beneath his brows. "What *was* he doing there? They're our pigs. What are these men doing here at all, and why was one of them killed?"

"They're Germans," said Callum. "You know that. They say that their friends are on the mainland, and that they have taken this island and it belongs to them now."

"This island? It's ours."

Callum said nothing, he felt in his pocket for his pipe.

"Callum," said the boy slowly.

"Yes, son?"

"Are they going to kill us?"

"Aye," said Callum; he could not find his pipe and he frowned. "They are going to shoot us. Ah, here it is," and he tapped the bowl of the pipe in the palm of his hand.

"Should I feel afraid, Callum?"

Callum began to prise at the cold ashes with his little finger. "Do you feel afraid?" he asked softly.

"Yes."

"It's all right," said Callum.

"But should I feel afraid, Callum? Isn't it wrong?"

"No, laddie," said Callum. "It's not wrong. I shouldn't believe you if you said you weren't afraid."

"But you're not afraid, are you?"

Callum looked thoughtfully at his pipe. "No," he said at last. "I don't think I am."

"But why? Why don't you mind if I'm afraid?"

"It's different, son. You see, you ought to live, and you know that, and you never thought you'd ever die. That's why it hurts. But with me it's different. There's so much for you to do, and you've never thought about dying, have you?"

The boy looked puzzled. "Sometimes. There was a bird up on the cliff once, with a broken wing. It was a big herring-gull, and when I climbed up to it I frightened it, and it ran away and fell over the edge. It couldn't fly and it fell down on to the Teeth and it was killed, because it didn't move and the sea washed it away. I saw it fall, and all of a sudden I wondered what it felt like, and I was frightened. It's like that now. I don't know what it will feel like."

Callum didn't answer, he had found his tobacco and was filling the pipe. He moved methodically, pressing each strand into the bowl, and sucking at the stem occasionally.

"Callum," said the boy, "will it hurt?"

The islander looked up the airman. Mann didn't move. "No," said Callum. "I don't believe it'll hurt. It's not that that hurts."

"What does hurt? Will they torture us, like cutting off a herring's tail and throwing it back?"

"No, not that."

"What is it then, Callum?"

"It's knowing they're wrong. It's knowing we're right and yet they can still take our island and kill us like this. It's knowing that they're evil, aye, more evil than the worst of us, and yet they can do what they want. It's knowing that just being right doesn't stop other people from being wrong and doing you harm."

The boy said. "That doesn't hurt me. But I wish we were strong like them and could stop them doing this."

"We're strong," said Callum. "We're very strong because we're right perhaps."

"But they're going to shoot us just the same, Callum, aren't they?"

"Yes."

"And you're not afraid?"

"No, that doesn't frighten me."

"Then," said the boy, "I'm not afraid either." And he challenged Mann with another stare.

Callum had lit his pipe and he spoke from behind its smoke. "Yes," he said, "tell yourself that, son."

"And it won't hurt."

"No, son, it won't hurt."

"I don't think they'll do it."

Callum said nothing.

"But I would have liked to see Bevan's wife with the sow she gets," said the boy. "And next year if Dad came home I was going to school on the mainland. I didn't want to go, but I'd like to go now."

Callum looked sad. "Yes," he said. "That's what I was trying to tell you." And they were both quiet for a long while.

"Then, Callum," said the boy, "after they've killed us, what will happen?"

"What do you mean?"

The boy frowned, "I mean what will happen to Mam, and the bitch who's going to have pups, and will Bevan's wife get her sow, and will it all be like it is, although we won't be there?"

"No," said Callum. "It'll never be the same now, because they won't be able to forget. It won't be the same for your mother because you won't be there and she'll suddenly realise how much you meant to her. And the bitch will have pups, but because she was your dog there'll be no one to look after them like you would do, and perhaps the pigs will get them. And Bevan's wife will get her sow, laddie, but it won't be the most important thing in her life as it was before these men came and killed her boy downstairs. And perhaps she'll sell the wireless to someone else, to me or Brian, because it will remind her too much of the boy. And when the women stand in the Gutter they'll remember that the

German's body lay there. And the children won't be able to play in the Hollow without remembering that the plane was burnt there, and it will figure in all their wee games. But that isn't what I mean." He took the pipe from his mouth and looked at it in disappointment. "It's gone out now," he said. "My old dad said a man shouldn't talk when he smoked, and he'd get very angry if folk expected him to. He said it was like praying, best done on your own in silence."

"What did you mean, Callum?"

"When I was a boy," said the islander, "I went to sea for the first time with my father, and stood at the tiller with him and hauled in the nets, you know how, son. We went out for a week in fine weather. The sea was calm and it rolled in gently as if it was fine to see us sailing there. And it was bright green like the grass is here in spring. And I was very proud and laughed at it because it was so calm. And I was proud of the boat because although it was only a little thing it could sit out there on the great ocean and do as it pleased. I knew I was the greatest thing there because I could sail on the sea for days and days and nothing happened to me." He stopped and the boy said, "Yes?"

"But the next time my father went out the weather was bad and he wouldn't take me. And the boat didn't come back in a great storm, greater than this. The waves came right up to the cottages, under the door, and washed away the jetty and tore out the lantern. And I knew that I had been wrong, laddie. The boat had been tender, she carried too heavy a sail, that the sea had been fooling me, that it could be evil and cruel, as well as calm and friendly."

"I don't understand what you mean," said the boy. "I know yon things."

"I don't know how to tell you," said Callum, "but you know these men now. You hadn't seen anything like them before, and, of course, you didn't know that men like them could be."

But the boy had lost interest, he was looking at Mann's heavy pistol.

"Will they shoot us with yon?" he asked, and before Callum could answer he went on, "But what will the airmen do afterwards?"

"They don't know what they'll do, though they'll have plans, oh aye, they'll have plans, for yon folk plan everything. But they don't know what they'll do because they don't know what our folk will do."

The boy lay back again, and turned his head to one side so that neither the islander nor the airman could see his face, and Mann knew that he was trying not to cry. The boy's face was white, and Mann hoped that he would cry because it would help him. The old man leaned forward and took the boy by the shoulder.

"Does it hurt much, laddie?" he asked.

The boy did not lift his head, he mumbled something that neither Mann nor the old man could hear, and then he moved his shoulder from beneath the islander's hand. His cheek was red on one side where it had been pressed against his arm.

"It wasn't anything," he said, and he turned and stared angrily at the navigator. "It wasn't anything."

And once again it was quiet, and only the storm pounding at the roof, the wind against the walls and down the drains in a hoarse whistle. The boy spoke sharply, quickly.

"I want to know what it's going to be like," he said. "I don't like feeling that nothing will happen here afterwards. I wanted to go to the mainland, and now I won't. I wanted to see whether Bevan's wife's sow has a litter. And I never shall."

"But when these things happen," said Callum gently, "they won't forget. They'll remember the four men that came down in a plane, and the boy they killed, and the dog. They'll remember the man dead in the Gutter, and then us. And people will think of us not as we are, a fisherman and a boy"—he smiled—"who wears out his clothes faster than his mother can repair them, but as someone they can point to and say, 'It might have been us, yon happened before we did anything!'"

"And will they know I was afraid?"

"Aye, they'll know, but they won't think about it like that. Perhaps some of them will think how terrible it was and thank God it didn't happen to them, but others will say 'See what's happening, yon's got to be stopped.' And they'll point us out to other people and say, 'How long are you going to let this go on? When are we going to stop it?' and perhaps at first they won't know how to stop it, but sooner or later they'll stop it."

"You mean we're like the saints?"

"No," said Callum softly, "because we're not saints. It might easily have been someone else. But because we're ordinary people the other ordinary people will see what is being done to them and say, 'We shall stop this!' "

"You mean the people on the mainland too?"

"Aye," said Callum, "they'll hear. And perhaps they'll be content with pitying us, or perhaps they'll forget us, for we're a long way away. But what happened to us will soon be more important than whether Bevan's wife gets her sow. That's what yon Germans don't realise. At first it's easy to conquer, but later it's hard to hold, because when they take us all together they canna hold us down any more than the sea can sink this island. But people have to see things for themselves, they canna be told all things. That's why I'm not afraid, laddie. I've told you now."

Mann got up quickly. He walked across to the window and the noise of his boots was loud and the boards creaked beneath them. The old man stopped talking, and he and the boy looked at the airman as he stood with his back to them, looking out through the dirty glass to the rain and the plume of foam floating above the cliff at the summit of the island. The island was the same as it had been since he came there. Through the flecks of dirt on the window, the dead flies that clustered on the edge of the pane, the cobwebs, and the aborting green thickness of the glass he could see it. Cottages, sturdy and white, crouching down into the heather, the patchwork of small fields rising up the hill, and above that the rolling slope with the grass turning and bowing before the wind, and all shining with rain, and, rolling over and over it all, the spray from the sea. The sky was grey, thickened to black here and there, and against it occasionally a fleck of brilliant white that Mann at first did not recognise. They were the gulls, flying up against the weather until the wind forced them down.

He knew the man and the boy were staring at him, and he wondered what they were thinking. He heard the boy whispering, and the old man replying, "I don't know, son."

He stood there for a long while looking at the island, his back to the prisoners and the hand behind it gripping the pistol, with a finger along the trigger guard. He would have liked to have spoken to the man and, above all, to the boy. He did not know why he wanted the boy to speak to him, but it had been so long since he had spoken to a child. There were things about this island he would like to have known, things that only a child could tell him. It would soon be dusk, and after that the night which would be followed by dawn, and at dawn the pilot said they must be shot. Mann hadn't been told that he would do it, but he knew that it would be him. He would shoot the boy first, and although the pilot insisted that it must be done where the rest of the islanders could see it happening, he would do it quickly before the boy knew it was happening. The pilot said that their bodies must be put in the Gutter.

He wondered if the woman would be watching, and realised suddenly how much he wanted to see her again. It wasn't like Hart. He felt that between them stood a gulf of misunderstanding, so much to explain, and he felt that somehow he was responsible for what Hart had done to her.

The wind changed again, and it now drove the rain against the window so that the view was bleared and without sense or proportion. Mann turned away from the window and went back to his seat. He took off his cap and laid it down beside him, and pushed his hand through his hair. He felt tired.

He realised how long he must have stood at the window, for the boy was asleep and breathing heavily into his sleeve. He lay with his head on his arms, and his body stretched out restlessly. His boots seemed so large and his jersey was a man's jersey, the collar was rolled down and the cuffs of his sleeves turned back over the wrists. The darns in the elbows reminded Mann of his own son, and his wife sitting in the big chair with her workbasket.

There was a noise, and he looked from the boy to the islander. Callum was standing up, and he was holding out his pipe to the navigator.

"If you don't mind it being mine," he said, "you can smoke it. I've just filled it."

Mann frowned. "No," he said; it was as if the islander had

sensed what he had been thinking, and he felt irritated. Callum put the pipe back into his pocket; he didn't seem put out by the refusal. "I thought you might want to smoke," he said, and sat down again. He put his hands in his pockets, across his belly, and looked up at the navigator.

"You don't mind if I talk to you?"

"If you want to."

"It's just that I want to ask some questions," said Callum, "if you don't mind. Things worry me. I know that you will shoot us, and it isn't that. Man, it's just that I don't understand why you, you in particular, do these things."

Mann looked at him suspiciously, "What do you mean?"

"When you brought that boy's body across to the cottage I noticed how gently you laid him on the couch, and how your anger rose up in you when we said we didn't want any more help. I think you were hurt then. And then I wondered why you saw how terrible it was for yon thing to have happened, and yet you seemed to think you had been right to do it."

"What does it matter to you what I think?" said Mann.

"Does it matter to you what *I* think?"

"Of course not."

"Man, I don't believe you," said Callum firmly. "You wanted to speak to Colin's wife when she came to you on the jetty."

Mann stood up angrily. "You told her to come?" He walked over to the window again and turned about quickly. "You sent her along hoping she'd get me to betray my friends?"

"No, man, no," said the islander patiently, as if he were still talking to the boy. "I knew she was coming, oh aye, she came and told me, and because I didn't know you, I said she shouldn't. But she did, just the same."

Mann sneered. "It's kind of you both to take an interest in me like this, but hardly in keeping with your present role. You're a conquered people, we don't want your help. We don't need it."

Callum did not answer right away, he stretched out his legs and looked down at his toes. "It wasn't for you. We wanted you to let *us* go."

"And you thought we'd do that?"

"Aye, we thought so then. It was simple then. We thought we

were the only prisoners on the island. You see, man, when you came we could see no difference between you all, yon fellow who's your officer, the man you found dead in the Gutter, the other man and yourself. You were all the same to us, just enemies we hated. When you came it was as if you walked down the brae with death in your small hands, and it didn't seem to us that any one of you was more to blame than the others. But as you stayed things changed."

"You're not making much sense."

"I'm a fisherman, and yon's a simple life. Until you came we didn't have to grapple with things, like you are making us do. But now I see we aren't the only prisoners, aye, if nothing else I see that. And the difference is that we know our jailers. You don't. Do you follow me, man?"

Mann's voice was harsh. "No."

"When you came we couldn't tell you apart, it wasn't just your fine uniforms, but you all sat behind yon guns and gave *us* orders, and seemed so grandly sure of yourselves, where to us everything was confused. You went about your pretty little business of murder and robbery, and it didn't seem strange to you. You had no decency, no godliness. You were all the same. Then we began to recognise you. There was your officer, he with the finest clothes of you all, and the little eagle on his breast. He gave the orders and sent the rest of you to do things. He made decisions, about the boat, our psalms, and shooting me and the laddie here. And we saw that he was different from the rest of you, he planned it all. And then we recognised the other man who was killed. He was easier to understand because he left all the responsibility to your officer. He laughed at us, and hit us, and molested Colin's wife as if he had every mortal right on his side. And then your friend, the wee mannie who gave the coin to the bairns, who stroked a dead dog and then fired his gun down into the shieling. When we looked out of our windows we would sometimes see him at work with his signs of the Cross and such godly devotions as he sat at the gun. And you . . ."

"Yes?" said Mann. He had not moved.

"Man, you are harder to understand, because you want to talk to us, but never listen to us, because you brought the boy's body

across and were tender with it. Because you speak our own
language and because you were kind to the boy here and didn't
hit him when he showed he hated you, like your friends might
have done. In all of you, man, we can see something that is a bit
of ourselves, and something that is a bit foreign. That is why I
wanted to talk to you, because it's not as easy as I thought. There
isn't just one of you. There are so many."

"And so?"

"So perhaps I see that you're the real prisoners. Your officer
boy doesn't mind, perhaps because he is his own jailer and built
the prison to suit himself. And the man who was killed didn't
mind because in prison he found more license than he might
outside. But you and the other man, although you don't know it,
are trying to escape. When he gave the children the coin he was
trying to get out, and then the wall closed in on him and he
fired the machine gun down into us. And you talked to Colin's
wife about your bairn and bird-nesting and your home, and then
the wall closes in about you too, and you shoot us."

He stopped. He had been talking to his boots, and now he
stopped and looked up at Mann. The navigator had not changed
his expression. He was frowning still and Callum wondered
whether he had been understood.

"That's how it seems to you," said Mann noncommittally.
"You're entitled to think that."

Callum smiled. "No," he said. "I know your creed better than
yourself, man. I'm not entitled to think anything more than that
you're right, for if I think you're wrong, man, I might try to stop
you doing the things you do."

"What we do is justifiable."

"Man, you're looking for easy answers," said Callum with a
rise in his voice. "That's why you do these things perhaps, it's
an easy way out. If I thought it didn't matter I wouldn't talk to
you. That you're going to shoot us doesn't matter even, although
it's harder for an old man to die than young men think. The boy
won't see the sow that's coming to the island, if you let it come
now. He'll never go to the mainland for school, and he'll not go
nesting in the cliff any more. Aye, it hurts me to think about that,
and while you were standing at the window I cried. But it isn't

only that. I know that some day you'll be defeated, some day your power'll be destroyed, some day all the evil will be crushed. I know it, man, I know it."

He took out his pipe and lit it slowly. While he did so Mann noticed how the wind seemed to have risen, how heavily the boy breathed into his woollen sleeve.

"You want me to go on?" asked Callum.

"Go on, you can't do any harm preaching."

"It isn't only those things," said Callum again. "Because the evil you do in the name of others has made you suffer, you yourself must help destroy it. It's a poor thing that has happened to this island, but it's part of a big thing that's going on wherever you and your guns go. Everywhere the people you oppress are doing what we've done on this island, they're resisting you, man, and sooner or later, but always sooner than you think, they'll be too strong and too many for you to kill. None of your fine prisons will hold them all, and because you and men like you are prisoners too—unless you want the prison to collapse and cover you, you must help tear at the stones from the inside."

Mann smiled, "You preach," he said, "and like most preachers you say nothing."

Callum didn't smile, he took the criticism seriously. "I don't often speak," he said. "I read the Bible on Sundays because we've no minister here. But there was little on this island to make us gossip until you came. Only the children chattered, because life was new and fresh, and so fine to a bairn. We weren't unhappy until you brought us the ugliness of your lives."

Mann felt that he should speak, should justify himself, and he raised his voice and spoke nervously. He felt angry, but it was not with the islander.

"You're right," he said. "You're right when you say that we do these things, but you don't understand why we must. You don't understand because you are isolated on this island, you don't understand why we have to do them. You don't understand because the sea is not like men's minds. With our strength we must be ruthless, and forget sometimes what you'd call kindness!"

Callum shook his head and leant forward on his knees earnestly.

"You don't forget," he said. "You canna. You carried the boy across when he was killed, and you saw how much sorrow his death had brought us. You didn't shoot Colin's wife when she left the cottage. You canna forget," he said again. "You canna forget kindness any more than you could forget an arm or a leg, but you bludgeon it until it's numb, or let some other body do it. And you go on striking at it because you're afraid of it."

"You don't understand," said Mann shortly.

"Man, I didn't," said Callum, "but I'm beginning to now, and perhaps I shall understand it all before you let them shoot me."

"Why do you say things like that?" shouted Mann angrily. " 'Before I let *them* shoot you.' As if I were not one of them. As if I were one of you."

"Which are you?" asked Callum quietly.

"We must stop talking now," said Mann, and his face set.

"Aye," said Callum, "we'll stop talking, but we'll both go on feeling and thinking just the same, won't we?"

The boy was awake. He had been leaning on his elbows listening to them without their knowing it, and when he spoke they started and turned to him.

"Why do you talk to him, Callum?" said the boy. "He's going to shoot us. Why do you talk to him?"

Callum pushed at his pipe again with a little finger. "Perhaps because he might be sitting here waiting to be shot, and me there with his pistol, and we'd be thinking just as we are now. Or perhaps it's because he has a son at home like you."

"He's six," said Mann, "and he's not as strong as the boy."

"Can he look after pigs?" asked the boy eagerly. "Can he climb the rocks, and has he been to sea?"

It was the first time Mann smiled. "No," he said. "He lives in the city where there aren't any rocks and pigs, and the only sea is in the docks. It's dirty there and full of the stuff that the sailors throw from the ships. But he'd like this island."

"I could show him a ledge where the herring-gulls nest," said the boy proudly. "A whole row of them, and the nests are full with young birds, and they sit there all day with their mouths open, making a din, and the mothers drop food in, and they fly down the Gutter to get it. I could show him a pool where you can get crabs as big as my foot, and another one where we swim, and another one that's too deep to see the bottom. and as black as Callum's Sabbath suit." He stopped, his voice became less shrill. "But I don't suppose I'd like him enough."

"He's never been nesting," said Mann, "but I think he'd like to go. I think he'd like you, too."

"I don't think I'd like him," said the boy again, and he dropped on his back again and pretended to go to sleep. Callum looked at Mann, but the navigator avoided his eyes.

"You lived in a city?" asked Callum.

"Yes, Hamburg," said Mann, and the mention of the name brought to him a vivid nostalgic picture of it. "I worked at the docks."

"I don't like cities," said Callum. "Have you always worked there?"

"No," said Mann. "When I was younger I lived by the Rhine, in a little town where my father had a butcher's shop. I played by the river with my sisters, and in the woods, and we went nesting too. But later we moved to Hamburg where my uncle got my father a job in the docks. He was killed in the troubles there after the war, and I went to work there. I married in Hamburg, and my son was born there. He's never seen the Rhine or the sea. That's why I think he would like this place."

"What's his name?"

"You'd call him Henry."

"No, we'd call him Harry."

Mann looked out of the window. It was getting darker. "It will soon be dusk," he said. The old man nodded and the navigator turned to him and said earnestly.

"If you'll tell the lieutenant who killed Hart and burnt the boats, I don't think he'll shoot the boy. He will shoot you, but you can save the boy's life."

"I don't know who killed him."

"You must know," said Mann impatiently. "You're the head of these people, you know them. You must know who would have done it?"

"Does it matter?" asked Callum. "Any of us might have. You want an easy answer again. Man, it *doesn't* matter! All of us

wanted to do it in a way. In a way all of us did do it, just as all
of you did that thing to Colin's wife. We bear equal blame, and
so do you unless . . ."

"Unless what?"

"Unless you break down that prison."

"You're being stupid," said Mann angrily. "You're sacrificing
a boy's life for nothing!"

"We don't think it's for nothing, no, it's not for nothing. The
boy is afraid, and there are so many things he'll not see now, but
we don't believe it's for nothing. You're wrong, you're all wrong,
and nothing will make you see that. You're trying now to make
things easier for yourself. But who speaks for *you*? Do you think
your officer has to bargain with us? It doesn't matter to yon
whether he shoots the right man or the wrong, so long as someone
is shot."

Mann shrugged his shoulders, he did not want to talk any more,
but when Grun came up to relieve him shortly afterwards he felt,
once more, the overpowering desire to talk. Grun stood in the
doorway, he looked drawn and white, and he stared nervously
at the islanders.

"The lieutenant wants you," he said. "Has there been any
trouble?"

Mann put his pistol in its holster. "They won't trouble you,"
he said.

"I don't understand them," said Grun, "sitting there, waiting,
just waiting until we take them out and shoot them."

"Don't you think they ought to be shot?" asked Mann suddenly.

Grun looked at him queerly. "You're asking a lot of odd
questions lately," he said. "Surely you don't expect us to let
them kill Hart and burn the boats and do nothing about it?"

"But the boy didn't kill Hart, and, after all, look what Hart did."

"I don't think you're using your head," said Grun, and he
came into the room and eased the top buttons of his tunic, taking
off his cap. "We haven't time to decide this or that. We've got to
make decisions quickly."

"*We* have?" said Mann with a little smile.

"You know what I mean."

"I don't know what you mean," said Mann irritably. "You try to fool me. One day you're the biggest coward and objector. Next day you're apologising and agreeing with everything that's done. You hate all this sort of thing, I believe. But you cling to it with a dirty, unpleasant fascination."

Grun stared at him. His mouth was open slightly.

"It's hard to talk to *you*!" shouted Mann, hating the look. "You shut yourself up in a little cage and are too frightened to say what you feel. You hate this rotten business, but go on doing your part of it."

"Well," sneered Grun, "what do you do?"

Mann's temper collapsed. "Nothing," he said.

Grun felt triumphant. "No," he said quickly, "because there's nothing to do. If we lose there's no hope. You've seen what these people would do to us, they'd have no more mercy than they have for Hart. Everywhere they'd like to tear our throats out, but men like you think you can get the best of both sides. While we're strong nothing will happen to us. Unless we talk like you!" He shouted the words and pointed at Mann.

"Oh stop acting!" said Mann. "Have you been drinking again?"

"It's not acting and it's not drink. I know all about this behind-the-hand talk of yours! We'd be all right with different leaders, and so on. But we'd be useless without them, so what good is it to say we've been wrong here or there? We couldn't do better. We've a strong leadership and with it we'll be safe. Why pity these people, we make special concessions to people of other races. . . ."

"Oh, stop lecturing," said Mann. "I've heard it all before. You're like an old record."

"Lecturing now! You're getting dangerous and someone should talk to you. You worry too much about these people and it doesn't help, it gets you in the end. They're all right. Even here on this island they're not like the Poles or the Slavs, and we'd treat them fairly well if they'd only be reasonable. You can't blame us when they turn on us."

"Yes," said Mann. "They've been most unreasonable. Grun, you must know you're talking nonsense."

"I know you," said Grun hysterically. "You think the old times were best, you're the weak link in the chain. . . ."

"If I thought you were trying to convince me and not yourself," said Mann, standing up, "I'd listen to you seriously. As it is, I'm going down."

Grun caught the navigator's arm. His voice changed. "Don't you see, Mann? Don't you see?" He looked over his shoulder. "There's nothing else we can do."

Mann looked across at Callum. The islander had been looking at them with deep interest, although he had not understood them, and the boy was still asleep, or pretending to be. Mann would have liked to ask the man for the pipe now, but he picked up his cap and put it on.

"Perhaps you're right," he said wearily. "It hardly matters now. I can't talk to you. There's nobody any more I can talk to." He looked stern. "Don't bother the old man and boy, let them sleep if they will."

II

THAT night the woman gathered as many islanders as she could in Callum's house. They made no pretence about going there, and Mann, sitting at the gun in the doorway, watched them going. He could see their shadowy figures through the rain and darkness, heard occasionally the closing of the door. and saw the gleam of light as it was opened. The storm seemed to be expending itself in one violent blow against the island. It was worse than it had ever been. The floor of the room was wet with driving rain and the cold bit into Mann's body. The wind rocked the gun between his knees and along the shifting shingle of the breach the waves roared incessantly.

Mann did not know why he made no attempt to stop the islanders, he was almost fascinated by the sinister significance of their gathering. The whole of his stay on the island seemed to be symbolised by the darkness and strength of the storm that night. Dark shadows in the rain, sly concealing movements, things that did not make their meaning clear, but clung to the shadow of night and anonymity. And he watched them without hindering because he felt that he could not stop what was to happen.

He saw the woman leave first for Callum's cottage, a shawl across her head, and he felt stirred by the poignancy of her life, and yet repelled by the force that she and her people there exerted upon him. And then after her came the others, with an occasional white face turned apprehensively towards the dark shape of the navigator sitting by the gun. He counted them, there must have been every adult on the island going to the little door.

In Callum's cottage the rain steamed from the heavy clothes and conversation was soft, the men stamped their feet and the women looked at one another with the rain-drops beaded on their round cheeks. They made no attempt to make themselves comfortable, but stood near the door, as if they were in a hurry to be gone as soon as possible. And they looked at the woman. She stood by Callum's wife, facing them timidly with her arms crossed beneath her breasts and the wide, smooth face marred by the slight frown above her eyes. Mann would have been alarmed by the look in the eyes, affected strangely by the softness of her hair, the generous sympathy of her figure.

"They'll shoot them to-morrow morning," she said abruptly, and laced and unlaced her arms nervously, looking quickly from one to others. And they in return watched her keenly, jostling by the doorway, and fussing with their clothes to relieve their feelings.

"They won't," said the man with the stick. "They're only fooling with us!"

"I know you canna believe it," she said, "but they'll shoot them to-morrow, unless we stop them."

"We know how you feel, lass," said one man, he was Callum's brother-in-law. "We feel it our own selves. Since they came we haven't been able to think, just feel, and we never knew we could hate so much. And they have kept us to our homes so that we have grown to hate the very walls God gave us for shelter. But they've guns and we canna stop them."

"Who murdered one of them?" said a rising voice. "That's why they do this, because one was murdered. We ought to know who did it. Let him confess it!"

"Do you want to give him up, now?" she flashed at him. "Do

you think it will make any difference? They'll shoot Callum, anyway."

"But one of us killed the man. The Lord said, Thou shalt do no murder. Who has sinned?"

She spoke passionately. "How can you talk about guilt? Does it matter now who killed him? They struck a blow at the poor boy at the wireless. I don't have to tell you surely? They came and killed a boy, they robbed us, destroyed our boats. They kill a boy's dog and then give him a coin for it all. They drive us into our homes, arrest us, shoot us. They tell us they mean us no harm, but *who are they*? What do they want? They don't care for us any more than we do for the herring we clean and gut. You don't talk about guilt when you think of them, you can only hate them!" She stood back until her shoulders rested against the wall, and her arms hung by her side. "And yet some of you cowardly bodies wanted to repair the boat and let them go!"

They shifted uneasily.

"Aye, they would have been gone now if the boat hadn't been burnt!" said a man's surly voice from the back.

"What are *you* thinking about?" she turned on him angrily, standing on her toes so that she might see him above the heads, and he moved behind the crowd out of her sight. "Not the bairns' dog up on the hill, not the boy by the wireless set, not Callum and the laddie over there waiting. No, my wee man, you're thinking about the boat you hoped to save while we let the others be destroyed."

He became angry then, and pushed his way through the islanders to her. He was short and sturdy, and dark behind a low-peaked cap. "Whoever burnt the boat should pay for it! Aye, it's fine to talk, but we're not the military. What are we going to do without boats when they've gone? Whose going to pay for them?"

"Go and get your money from the Germans!" she said scornfully. "Perhaps they'll pay you to row the small boat across for them. Go and tell them Callum burnt the boat!"

Another man stepped out, he took a pipe from his mouth and spat in the fire. "We shouldn't be quarrelling," he said briefly. "Let's hear what the lass has to say."

"Don't you see?" she asked earnestly. "They think we're the prisoners, but that is na' true. They canna get away, the small boat will na' carry them beyond the foreland. They canna do anything but bully us with their guns. *They're* the real prisoners. They're locked on this island with us, and the sea and the storm and our own selves can see they don't escape. The sea isn't feared of them, but we are. For how long? So long as we let them go on shooting and starving us. *So long as we let them!*"

"It's easy to talk, lass," said a woman sarcastically. "I suppose we should go over and ask them to give themselves up, and then wait for the boat to come out from the mainland." She pulled the baby higher up her arms and covered its face with a shawl. "How *can* we stop them. They have starved us, they've taken all the food we had for themselves. They've taken our husbands and our sons. They'll shoot us. How can we stop them?"

"We can stop them," said the man who had spat into the fire. "Go out to them to-morrow. I don't care what they do, but when they come out we must stop them. What's the matter with us?"

"Yon's not easy," said the woman from the wall, and the frown had deepened above her eyes. "They're strong outside, only weak in their poor souls. They don't trust themselves, but their guns have no souls."

"You canna talk about them like that," said the man whose boat had been burnt. "We don't know them, they don't act like human beings. Yon talk about destroying them is daft. They could kill us all. They have no need to keep us alive."

"There are stones on the shore," said a third man. "When I was a bairn I threw one at a herring-gull and killed it. They can kill a man if they're well thrown."

"I don't know how we can stop them," said the woman, and she now stood listlessly by the wall. "But to-morrow morning we must be there, and when they begin we shall know how to stop them."

She leant back against the wall, her anger had spent all her strength, and she could hardly realise that she had been speaking, that all these things had so suddenly, so violently interrupted her life. But she knew that what was to happen was right.

"All of us must be there," she said, but in a voice so low that no one heard it above the storm.

"Let us sing a psalm," said Callum's wife. "Let us sing whether they like it or not. They canna frighten us now."

The concertina was brought from the shelf above the fire, and Mann across the way heard its first whistling notes and then the words with which he was now so familiar.

"Behold how good and pleasant it is for brethren to dwell together in unity. . ."

He moved restlessly at the gun and longed for dawn.

III

THE pilot found that the morning suited him very well. There was a gleam of orange to the east and he knew that the storm had broken. He shaved very carefully, passing the razor several times across the cleft in his chin and humming gently to himself as he listened to the radio. The news had been good. Heavier raids by his comrades, success, and now, for them on this island, the end of the storm. The wind had been dropping since midnight, when, suddenly, at the height of its fury, it veered away out to sea and tore at the waves as it passed. But the storm was dying and the pilot looked out of the window with satisfaction. To sail in the dinghy was a risk, but it was a risk he understood.

He wiped the razor on a scrap of paper and looked reflectively at the fold of lather there. He felt his chin and nodded. His humming became louder.

He dressed slowly and methodically, smoothing the medal ribbon, rubbing the dust from his boots with the edge of the table-cloth. He looked with contempt at the pictures on the mantelpiece, the yellow photographs, and upstairs he heard the stirring of the prisoners.

He had been so preoccupied with the thought of the boat that he had almost forgotten them. It would be easy, of course, to take the boat and go now, the islanders could do nothing. But logically he could not see the sense in it. It was regrettable that Hart should have been killed, he told himself, as he combed his hair and brushed the moustache he had at last allowed to grow, but it wasn't just that he had been killed. It had been a blow struck by the enemy, and coming from the enemy it had to be returned far more forcefully, far more successfully.

The pilot realised that the situation was not without its irony. An airman had raped a girl, had had his skull crushed in, and his body thrown among the water where these people gutted their miserable fish. A bold thing to do, yes, but to leave the gun on its side on the beach was the act of children who did not know what they were doing.

The pilot sang a few words of the song played by the radio, and cursed the atmospherics that spoiled the reception of the melody, cursed the small mirror that did not give him a fuller view of himself that morning, and adjusted his cap smartly. He had not eaten that morning. He had not allowed Grun to leave the gun to make breakfast, and because of that his stomach rumbled resentfully. He realised that his body, in contrast to his spirit, felt a little weak.

After the hostages had been executed, they would leave. He didn't expect the islanders to produce the murderer now, and it didn't really matter. He had had to abandon the idea of burning the cottages: now that the storm was dying the smoke would alarm the mainland. The radio would be destroyed: the pilot had heard of messages being sent by oscillation, and to leave behind such a piece of technical equipment in the hands of these people would be stupid. He would suggest that the island be bombed when he returned.

The pilot felt the warmth of satisfaction. He looked down at his small feet and moved across the room once or twice, stepping in time to the music. For a long time, since the days he had first flown over Madrid in a fighter, he had felt that his ability had never yet been seriously tested, and because of that he had never really given himself up to the pleasure enjoyed by such men as Stern. The test had come now, and he was passing through it, he told himself, with commendable success. Now pleasure would be justified.

Stern! It was unfortunate that Stern had not lived to experience this, but he would have monopolised the credit and probably bungled the whole thing, anyway. There had been bungling enough. Grun! And Mann! The pilot still didn't know what to make of Mann.

He folded up his log book and placed it inside his tunic, and then he went to the door and opened it. Grun sat at the gun. His face was drawn, and the pilot noticed with irritation that the wireless operator was nervous and frightened. His eyes were heavy and his mouth twisted, and he was clutching the rosary in one hand.

"Put that thing away," said the pilot sharply, "and go up and tell Mann to bring the man down. I want to question him."

He closed the door and sat down in his chair, studying his boots for some minutes. There was a knock and Mann came in. The islander was with him, he had his hands in his pockets, and the pilot shouted at the navigator angrily.

"Why aren't his hands tied, Mann?"

"You gave me no orders."

"Do you have to wait for orders?"

Mann made no reply, and the pilot did not expect one. He studied Callum carefully. The man was not afraid, there was no false arrogance in his manner as he stood there, with his hands across his stomach and his big head drooping forward slightly on his chest. He was perfectly calm.

"Mann," said the pilot, "I want you to interpret carefully what we say. Tell him that he can expect justice, that we are not inhuman, and that we are prepared to bargain with him. He must realise that we hold the authority and that any concession on our part will be one of great generosity."

Mann repeated the statement, and after that the pilot and Callum spoke through him as if he had no senses, no thoughts of his own. He echoed them dispassionately, but could scarce control the stifling feeling that wanted to burst inside him.

"What do you want?" said Callum.

"We are prepared to spare the life of one of you, perhaps both," said the pilot briskly, "in exchange for some information. For example, details of the shipping lanes within range of this island. Give me a pencil," he said to Mann. "Now?" and he looked up at the islander with an eyebrow raised and the pencil resting on the paper.

"Perhaps it is fine play to joke with us," said Callum, "but if you're serious you must know that you're wasting your time. We're ordinary folk and we know little or nothing of what you want. Nor would I tell you if I did."

"It's madness to sacrifice your life when it's offered to you. Reasonable men don't go in for such heroics."

"Our lives mean nothing to you. You can take mine, or give it to me as you wish. But you're going to take it, I know. You must, because you canna afford mercy now, you've cut it out of your lives for so long. You've got to kill us."

The pilot looked up at Mann, as if he held the navigator responsible for the sentences he had just translated. Then he broke the pencil irritably between his fingers.

"Perhaps I was wrong," he said, and he stood up and leaned on his knuckles. He was very angry. "By your barbarism, your murderous attack on my man, you have absolved me from any pity or compassion my nature might have held for you. Although you stand close to us, perhaps, in blood relationship, when you oppose us with such behaviour you deserve no more consideration than a Jew or a Negro. You need lessons, lessons from an uncompromising teacher. When we hang you, for we shan't shoot you now, it'll be a lesson that the people we are generous enough to leave alive on this island will not forget!"

The old man was trembling. "Aye," he said. "When we die it will be a lesson. Before you came few people in the world knew us. All over the country they ate the fish we dragged from the sea, but they did not think of the fine men that caught them, and perhaps we did not think of them either. There was a gulf between us. But when you came and did what you've done, you bridged the gap, and across that bridge the ordinary folk come to fight you.

"You'll hang us," he went on, "you'll hang us on this wee island where the sea breaks, and others elsewhere in lands where they speak a tongue I don't understand, but still feel the things I feel; where there are laddies who like swimming and nesting and looking after an old sow; where there are young lassies full of compassion and tenderness; where there are men to be stirred by the devil in men like you. Everywhere you go you must hang them, but you don't know why you have to. You think, maybe, it's because you're strong, and being stronger must have no mercy for the weak, and so you go on killing us because, according to the likes of you, we don't deserve much else."

Callum moved forward to the table and looked straight at the officer. "But, mark me, man, you must kill us all if you want to be really triumphant, until there is no one in the world but yourselves, and that you canna do. You don't realise that wherever you go the hatred of you rises up behind you, and because of that there's no hope for you. Hatred canna be idle, it looks for something to occupy its hands, and it will use them against you. You can kill some of us, but the people aren't dying, their strength and life grows with every one of them you murder, even in your own country. No, it is *you're* dying, and your death follows you faster than you maybe think. No boat can carry you from that!"

The lieutenant's mouth drooped a little as he heard that much that Mann had been able to translate. The wisp of hair above his mouth was incongruous, and he closed his lips quickly and flung the broken pencil from him.

"Bring the boy down," he said. "I've been wasting time."

IV

I⸱T had stopped raining and the pilot stood outside the cottage with his hands on his hips, looking up, as if he were watching the slow drift of the clouds to the west. Behind him the waves were high, but the tide was ebbing, and with it their strength. On the embers of the burnt vessel the water glistened in many tiny beads. The pilot pursed his lips and looked up at the sky, at the gulls rising in circles and filling the air with their voices, but he was studying the cottage roof intently, and when he had examined it he blew out his lips and shook his head. He walked briskly to the end of the cottage and looked at the jetty. The storm had washed over it and systematically cleaned out the pointing that earth and sand had made between the stones. From each crevice there ran a chuckling stream of water, and the erection that Mann and Grun had built against the wind had gone. The sea had taken the tarpaulin away.

By the shore end of the jetty was a standard, ten or twelve feet high, that had once held a lamp, and it pointed its thin arm out to sea. When the pilot saw this he gave a sharp, satisfied intake of breath and slapped his thigh. The wind fluttered out the edges of his tunic and tightened it across his shoulders.

From their windows the islanders watched him, watched him call and saw Mann leave the cottage. The pilot pointed to the post and went inside, leaving Mann standing there, still looking at the post, capless, with the wind in his hair and the top three buttons of his tunic loosened. He made a lonely figure against the wind and seemed lost against the sky. He remained looking at the post for some time before he turned and followed the pilot inside.

The woman left the cottage first. She came to the door and stood there with a shawl drawn loosely about her shoulders. Her head was held high, and Mann, who had glanced through the window at her, noticed the length of her neck, and the brown of her skin in the bright light. He stood staring at her, and wondering what she would do. The wind, that had once driven itself brutally against the island, now drifted across its face and gently moved the woman's clothes about her figure. She hesitated in the doorway, glancing at the other cottages, but none of the doors opened. It was as if they withdrew from her. Then she pulled at her shawl with one hand and walked out some yards before her home and stood there resolutely. Mann glanced at Grun. The gunner was watching the woman with his eyes wide and his mouth relaxing. His hand moved automatically to the cocking piece of the gun.

"Let her alone," said Mann quietly, "she can do no harm."

Grun looked up quickly, but, unable to return Mann's stare, and surprised by the firmness of the navigator's face, he looked away. The woman did not move. Mann could almost sense the confusion of her feelings beneath the calm of her face. He wondered what the pilot would say. Airmen and woman stared at each other and the wind drove softly between them and the gulls rose higher and higher in the air.

Presently another door opened and a man and woman stood there. They took a pace or two from the step and then stopped, looking first at the woman, and then staring cautiously at Grun and the gun. The wireless operator fidgeted nervously. He did not look at Mann, but bit his lip and moved his feet with impatience.

"Now what?" he said jerkily.

"Leave them alone," insisted Mann. "They can do no harm. They've come to watch, that's all."

"Why don't they stay inside," said Grun. "They'll go if I fire." And he eased himself forward and pulled back the cocking handle.

"*Let them alone!*" said Mann firmly and he bent down and grasped Grun roughly by the shoulder.

"But the lieutenant . . ."

"*I'll take the responsibility!*"

Grun shrugged his shoulders. "All right," he said. "They're a cold-blooded lot."

"Just let them alone," repeated Mann.

The man and his wife left the step of their home and joined the woman in the open. She did not look at them, but her face flushed happily. They were wearing unaccustomed clothes, stiff and creased, clothes that were, Mann realised, their best. The man's suit was dark, single-breasted with all the buttons fastened, and he wore a high, starched collar. His hair had been smoothed with water and his face was red from recent shaving. He looked uncomfortable, and his arms hung loosely from the shoulders in embarrassment. And before him and his wife the woman stood with her blouse brilliantly white, and her legs sturdy in black stockings that had a tiny hole above the right ankle.

And soon from each cottage more of them came, some in their seamen's jerseys and high boots, but most in their best clothes, and none wore hats, except the old man with the querulous stick, and he wore a high, black bowler. Beneath his arms he carried a big book, its pages red-edged and its covers tipped with brass.

Mann felt fascinated by the scene. There were no children there, but in one of the cottages a baby was crying, and it went on crying. All the men were old. Their hair was white or grey, and the woman was the youngest there. She looked like a happy girl, her lips were parted in a soft smile.

And behind this black and white group, sitting on its haunches was a black and white collie, with a red tongue flopping joyously from its open jaws.

Grun began to get excited. He got up and turned to Mann heatedly. "It's all very well to say let them alone," he said. "But what do they want, coming out and standing there as if they were going to church? I don't like it. Call the lieutenant or I'll fire at them!"

Mann hit him deliberately across the cheek. "Sit down," he said, "and let them alone, they'll do no harm."

Grun turned white. "It's all over," he said. "It's no good now." And he sank down by the gun and watched the islanders dejectedly. He seemed dwarfed by the slender length of the machine-gun, with its perforated radiator and brown leather belt.

The pilot came out and looked through the door way at the islanders. He was not surprised to find them there, and then he laughed shortly, dispensing with the joke as soon as he could.

"They're early," he said. "Did you find the rope?"

"There's some upstairs."

"Get it and bring the prisoners to the jetty. Grun, stay here at the gun. Let them sing their hymns," he said. "We can afford to be generous."

When they brought Callum and the boy into the open the boy saw the islanders and began to cry. He just let the tears fall down his cheeks and turned his back on them and walked with Callum to the standard. Mann had the rope coiled about his arm, and he felt that the walk to the jetty was taking hours. The wind was pushing against him, the stones and the sea receding as he walked. The pilot walked beside him briskly, without emotion, confident.

He stopped by the post and looked up at the metal arm.

"It will do," he said, and motioned to Mann.

Mann dropped the rope at his feet. Something was swelling up within him, and he could hardly see. He seemed conscious of every part of his body, as if the eyes of a great crowd were staring at him critically. The pilot's figure became blurred and lost in the sparkle of the waves. The storm was breaking, the clouds splitting and racing toward the darkness of the retreating storm, and behind them the sun rose majestically.

Mann couldn't speak. He looked at the pilot and shook his head.

The pilot's face seemed to tighten. At the corners of his eyes, his mouth, the wrinkles disappeared and the face lost its indifferent expression. He eased his neck nervously in the collar of his tunic, and pulled at the edges of his tunic. He opened his mouth, and Mann saw the tongue curl, but heard nothing.

"Herr Leutnant," he said, "I can't do this."

The pilot pulled at his pistol and pointed it at Mann. The navigator wanted to laugh, the tight feeling inside his chest loosened and his tongue became coherent.

"You won't shoot," he said. "You can't shoot, there'll only be you left if you do."

The pilot said nothing, but stood there with his arm and the pistol stretched out from his body. Mann pushed at his hair and began to speak quickly.

"Listen," he said. "You don't mean anything to me. When we came here we were the crew of a bomber, and tied tightly together by many things. But something has broken all that, and even now I don't know what it is. I don't owe you anything," he said earnestly. "Don't you see? *I don't owe you anything.*"

"Mann!" was all the pilot said.

"No," said the navigator.

The pilot glanced over his shoulder to the crowd. They had not moved. His arm dropped and he did not raise it again. Still half-glancing at the islanders, he said urgently, "Be sensible, Mann! If we show any weakness these people will tear us to pieces."

Mann could see the faces of the islanders, they seemed so much nearer. And the white stain of the woman's blouse was against their black clothes.

"They will," he said. "But I see it now. I've followed you, or men like you, for years because I didn't trust myself. Now I do, and you're asking me to give it up again. I can't, because I've got to take the chance. Once I was certain that without you I was nothing, but that with you people like me could be something. I relied on you, and through the years you strengthened that reliance by taking everything from me and giving me nothing. . . ."

"*Mann!*" said the pilot again, but the navigator went on:

"I thought that power, and dignity, and strength could be got only through you. But all you've given me is a hangman's rope."

"What are you talking about?" said the lieutenant thickly.

"And when there was evil," went on Mann, racing through the words, "evil like this that sickened me, I comforted myself with the thought that the responsibility wasn't mine, but yours, and even you could make mistakes. But these people," and he waved at the islanders, "don't make fine distinctions like that. You've made something out of me, and hundreds like me, something that we never recognise until moments like this. You say we're lost without you. But it isn't so, without us *you're* lost. So long as we let you, you will live, and going on doing the things you've been doing for years. Just so long as we let you!"

The pilot became excited. "Once more . . ." he said hysterically.

"No!" said Mann fiercely. "You see it's there. You won't shoot me, because without me you're lost. Without me there's no one to shoot, to bully and torment these people. There's no one to row that dinghy. And Grun is weak, when he sees I've deserted you you won't be able to do anything with him."

"How much have they paid you?" said the pilot. His voice was so choked that Mann could hardly understand him.

"They've paid me nothing," he said. "I don't know what they'll do with me. . . . But *you* haven't got me now."

The pilot stepped back, his feet slipped on the greasy stones. He staggered and the gun dropped from his hands and was sucked down by the waves. Mann heard the islanders singing, their voices were forced, but they were singing loudly. He looked at them. They were walking up to the jetty. The old man had taken off his bowler and held it loosely in one hand, in the other was an open book. Before them the collie danced in bounding side-steps.

Mann heard Grun shouting a warning, and for a moment the crowd stopped and the singing wavered. Then they moved forward again. Grun shouted once more, and the navigator held his breath and waited for the burst of fire. He felt cold, and he had forgotten the officer. He did not know that the man was on his knees on the edge of the jetty, reaching down, trying to grasp the pistol when the waves drained from it. Mann seemed to have no importance at all now, all the strength and passion had been sucked out of him. He was waiting for the gun to open fire.

But it did not, for around the corner of the cottage stumbled Grun, his coat open and his head bare. He was running clumsily, slipping, and glancing now and then over his shoulder. He ran toward Mann, hardly noticed the officer, he was shouting something that the navigator could not understand above the singing that had now risen enthusiastically.

Everything seemed to lose proportion among the noise of voices and the dog barking. Grun fell again as he reached the jetty, and he scuffled on his knees along the stones until he came to Mann. The navigator felt him grasp his tunic.

The pilot stood up. His face was white and the knees of his breeches were wet, his hands green with slime. Mann turned on him.

"You see?" the navigator said. "You *see*?"

He stepped forward. He did not know what he was going to do, and the pilot, startled by the movement, stepped back. He lost his footing and fell off the jetty. He rolled in the stones and the sea washed over him. He stumbled to his feet, his clothes wet and his hair over his face.

He began to run from the jetty, staggering up the beach toward the Gutter. For a moment, above the noise of the waves, there was the dragging sound of his feet through the stones. The islanders stopped singing to watch, and Mann and Grun watched too.

The collie sprang away, leaped from the jetty and bounded away after the pilot, barking wildly, its tail streaming out behind it. From among the islanders a man jumped down from the jetty and began to run after the dog, or so it seemed, for he whistled as he ran, and his sea-boots plunged heavily in the stones. But then he passed the barking animal and ran on to the pilot who was now floundering at the foot of the Gutter. The islander stood over him, with his hands on his hips, waiting for the pilot to get up.

Mann felt sick. He was trembling and hardly knew what he had done, and he stared stupidly down the beach to where the pilot crouched panting on the stones. He felt shaken by the absurdly ridiculous figure the pilot made. And then the islanders began to move towards Mann, singing their psalm again, triumphantly:

"*Behold how good and pleasant it is for brethren to dwell together in unity . . .*"

THE ELWY VALLEY, 1942–1943